Winner of the Atta Galatta Bangalore Literature Festival Book Prize 2023, and the Binod Kanoria Children's Book Award, 2023, **Mallika Ravikumar** is a lawyer-turned-writer, published by Penguin, Hachette, and Karadi Tales, amongst others. Apart from writing about law and history, she loves learning about trees, conducting tree walks, and creating videos about trees on her YouTube channel, *Tree Talk with Mallika Ravikumar.* To find out about her books, tree-walks and talks, and to learn more about the M4 series of legal mysteries published by Talking Cub, visit www.mallikaravikumar.com. You can reach Mallika on Instagram at mallika.ravikumar and treetalkwithmallikaravikumar.

Also in the series:

The Case of the Vanishing Gods

An M4 MYSTERY BOOK 2

THE CASE OF THE Missing TURTLES

MALLIKA RAVIKUMAR

talking CUB
An Imprint of Speaking Tiger Books

TALKING CUB
Published by Speaking Tiger Books LLP
125A, Ground Floor, Shahpur Jat,
Near Asiad Village, New Delhi - 110 049

Published in Talking Cub by Speaking Tiger Books in paperback in 2024

ISBN: 978-93-5447-751-5
eISBN: 978-93-5447-995-3

10 9 8 7 6 5 4 3 2 1

Typeset in Lora by Jojy Philip
Printed at HT Media Ltd, Greater Noida

To wildlife warriors around the world,
for giving a voice to the voiceless

'The Indian subcontinent is in an extinction freefall right now. The species we are losing are in fact the "maintenance engineers" of the ecosystems that keep us alive.'

—Bittu Sahgal
Conservationist and Founder,
Sanctuary Nature Foundation

Contents

1

Arrested

'Mirchi, help!' a shrill voice echoed down a narrow lane of Anand Nagar. 'Help! The police have arrested Appa!'

Curious heads popped out of windows; scampering children halted their games; jobless boys stared from the corner paan-shop.

'MIRCHI!' the desperate voice called again, this time accompanied by frantic knocking on a tin door.

'Shimplya!' Mirchi's grandmother emerged from the little house, her hands caked with flour. 'Kya baat hai?' she asked the little fellow dressed in a pale white shirt and brown shorts.

'Mirchi,' the boy panted, resting his hands upon his knees.

'He isn't home,' said the old woman. 'Check at Aslam bhai's shop...'

Shimplya was gone in a flash. Ever since Mirchi, the local scrap-collecting boy, had shown up at school one rainy morning in a big police car, accompanied by the Senior Superintendent of Police (SSP), his stature had sky-rocketed in Anand Nagar and the bastis nearby. Dozens had come to inquire about the matter, gripped by burning curiosity; but the story of Mirchi teaming up with the SSP's children to solve a high-profile crime during the summer continued to remain a secret. The details were known only to the families and close friends of the M4—the happening team of young detectives in the unhappening town of Maulsari. Few people, however, dared to get on the wrong side of Mirchi anymore—it had been months since the headmaster reminded him he was a sweeper's son; no teacher ever chided him for drinking water from the common water-cooler; even Aslam Malik, the scrap-dealer, bargained warily with Mirchi, giving him the best possible rate for his scrap. And for young boys like Shimplya, Mirchi had become an overnight hero, the go-to person in times of trouble, and the reason for Shimplya's frenzied late-afternoon search.

'Mirchi! Mirchi!' Shimplya ran down to Aslam bhai's shop. 'Mirchi!' he gasped, glad to finally spot his friend in a bright yellow shirt. 'I need your help!'

Mirchi held out his hand, motioning for Shimplya to wait, his attention consumed by the weighing scale upon which he'd placed a large pile of flattened cardboard cartons.

'Mirchi, sunn na,' begged Shimplya, tugging Mirchi by his arm as Munna, Mirchi's black mongrel, sniffed him up. 'It's urgent.'

'Kya hai?' asked Mirchi, as the weighing scale before him rocked to a halt.

'Appa has been taken by the police!'

'What for?' Mirchi nodded at Javed, Aslam bhai's buck-toothed assistant popularly known as Fawda, to weigh the next lot.

'I don't know. They wouldn't tell us.'

'But they've got to tell you!' said Mirchi, having learnt a thing or two about the law while solving their first case a few months ago. 'The police have to inform a person about the reason for his arrest.'

His sorry eyes pinned upon Munna's long pink tongue, Shimplya merely shook his head.

'Tell me,' Mirchi reached into the pocket of his khaki-coloured shorts, keeping an eye on the weighing scale. 'Have they taken him for questioning or did they arrest him?'

'I don't know. They just dragged him out of the house and stuffed him into the police van and sped away.' Shimplya wiped the tears from his eyes and the snot from his nose on the sleeve of his shirt.

'Alright.' Mirchi handed in the change, pocketed the notes given to him by Aslam bhai and turned to leave. 'Calm down and tell me what happened,' he put an arm around his troubled friend, as Munna trotted along.

'The police took Appa away,' Shimplya began sobbing as they walked. 'Mirchi, he has done nothing wrong.'

'Stop weeping like a baby,' Mirchi clicked his tongue. 'And tell me exactly what happened!'

'Appa returned this morning from a twelve-day fishing trip. He...he...he was tired and wanted to rest. After lunch, he went to sleep. At about three o'clock, there was a knock on the door... It was the police,' Shimplya paused as they turned the corner.

'"We are looking for Surmai Jadhav," the police announced. There were three of them. Aaji told them he was sleeping. They brushed her aside and burst through the door. Appa awoke in the commotion.

'"Are you Surmai Jadhav?" they asked. Appa nodded. Before anyone could say anything, they picked him up and dragged him out of the house. Aaji and Aai and I screamed, following behind them but they packed him into a police jeep and drove off.'

'But they must have said something!' Mirchi threw up his thin arms as they walked on. 'About why they were taking him.'

'We all kept asking. Aaji begged them to tell us. Aai kept saying we were poor fisherfolk. But they beat Appa with a stick and took him away like he was some criminal.'

Mirchi exhaled hard. In this respect, life in the fishing colony at Anna Nagar, where Shimplya lived, was no different from Anand Nagar, where he stayed.

There too, the police could rough up people under the pretext of questioning them. It did not startle him, but it certainly angered him. 'Then? Did any of you go to the police station and find out?'

'Of course!' Shimplya nodded. 'The whole neighbourhood—we followed behind on our bikes. But even there, we were brushed aside and asked to leave. Nobody told us anything at all.'

'And did you see your father there?'

'No! We couldn't see him. They wouldn't allow us to go inside.'

Stopping at the tea-shop at the end of the lane, Mirchi looked up at the sky. 'It must be nearly four,' he said. They didn't have much of the day left.

'Appa has done nothing wrong, Mirchi,' tears stung Shimplya's eyes again. 'He couldn't have! I know he couldn't have!'

'Ok chal,' Mirchi placed his empty sack upon his parked cycle and took it off its stand. 'Come with me.'

'Where?' Shimplya scratched his thick mop of hair as Munna hopped into the cycle basket.

'To the SSP Sahib's bungalow!'

2

Quest for Answers

'So, they just took your father away without giving a reason?' gasped Meera, sitting astride the balustrade of the porch outside her house in olive-green overalls, Rubik's cube in hand.

Shimplya nodded, awkward to be standing outside a huge bungalow in a posh place like Customs Colony.

'And you say Shimplya's father is a simple fisherman who could have done nothing wrong?' Meera turned to Mirchi.

Eyes on the colourful cube, Mirchi's square head bobbed from side to side.

'Which police station?' asked Malhar from the grassy patch outside the porch, as he undid his cricket gloves and bent down to cuddle an excited Munna, even as Meera tried making sense of Mirchi's head-shake; she could never quite tell if it meant a yes or a no.

'Sikka Chowki Police Station,' replied Shimplya softly.

'Woof!' Munna's ears stiffened. As a member of the M4, he was alert to all key sounds and smells.

'Damn! That's Inspector Shevre's police station,' cursed Malhar, dusting blades of grass off his prized Kohli jersey.

Rubbing the soft white patch on Munna's neck, Meera recalled their brush with Inspector Shevre during the previous investigation which she'd labelled *The Case of the Vanishing Gods*. The thought of Velu, a hapless plumber being beaten mercilessly at the police station under Inspector Shevre's watch, sent a shiver down her spine. But she said nothing, to avoid adding to Shimplya's worries. 'So... what do we do?'

'We going police station,' said Mirchi matter-of-factly, greatly emboldened by the pat on the back he'd received from the SSP for his courage in cracking the last case.

'But what do we ask?' Meera slid a hairband over her short hair. 'And why will Inspector Shevre tell us anything?'

'What choice do we have?' shrugged Malhar. 'Speaking to Baba is pointless. He will say what he always says *beta, don't interfere in police matters...* Let the police do their job. You know that!'

'Hmm...' Meera's sharp eyes narrowed. They couldn't possibly help Shimplya without knowing why his father had been arrested. 'Ok,' she nodded. 'Let's go, but...' she paused, remembering how they had sought help from their father's bumbling orderly, the last time they'd wanted to make enquires at the police station, 'Let's ask Murli kaka to take us.'

'You can't tell him you've got another school project,' said Malhar with a roll of his big almond-shaped eyes, referring to the excuse they'd conjured up to get the potbellied constable to escort them earlier.

Meera walked up to the uniformed guard who was fiddling with his mobile phone by the door. 'Murli kaka, we're hungry. Can you please take us to that halwai shop opposite Sikka Chowki Police Station for pakodas?'

'Pakodas?' Constable Murli's face lit up, as he licked his lips. 'And who are these two boys here?'

'Don't you recognize our friend Mirchi?' asked Meera.

'Of course! Of course! The boy who Sahib accompanied to school. Who doesn't know him? He is famous!' Murli kaka patted Mirchi's dry brown mane. 'And who is this fellow?' he asked, turning his nose up and stepping away from Shimplya.

'This is Mirchi's friend,' replied Malhar, not wanting to divulge too many details.

'A fisher boy?' Murli kaka remarked contemptuously. 'One can tell by just standing within a few feet of these people! So, are these friends going to join you for pakodas as well?'

'Yes! We will ride behind you on our cycles,' said Meera, not wanting to waste any more time.

'Quickly then,' Constable Murli hopped onto his motorbike. 'Before they run out of pakodas!'

3

Digging Deeper

'Since we're here...' Meera eyed the police station across the street, 'perhaps we could say hello to the inspector we met when we'd visited the police station for my summer project.'

'Inspector Shevre?' Constable Murli nodded, chomping on steaming hot onion pakodas.

'Yes, I think that was his name,' Meera pretended she'd forgotten, and quickly asked that her pakodas be packed into a takeaway parcel.

'Hmm... perhaps, we could drop in for a few minutes,' Constable Murli glanced at his watch.

Instructing Munna to wait by the cycles outside the gate, the children ran across the road towards the police station, Constable Murli following reluctantly behind them.

The place looked exactly as Meera and Malhar remembered it from the summer—compound walls lined with pink bougainvillea, bats hanging overhead from tall trees, an overpowering stench of bat-excreta, tin porch leading into a dingy black stone building. They examined the dozen odd faces outside, asking Shimplya if any of them was their father. He shook his head, and they marched straight in.

A great many people were inside the main hall. Some were standing by the door, others seated on their haunches along the wall, still others waiting on the bench. Three uniformed policemen were at their desks, one noting something into a large register, another peering into a computer screen, a third talking into his phone as a smiling Gandhi, stately Nehru, and stoic Patel watched over them from photo frames pinned to the wall.

'I think...Inspector Shevre...not on duty now,' Constable Murli surveyed the faces.

Pleased to hear that, Meera walked in boldly. 'Perhaps Inspector Shevre is inside. Let's wait a while,' she said, pointing out the lock-up to Shimplya, beckoning him to take a look inside. 'It would be so rude if he got to know that we were here and left without meeting him!'

'Let me go and see,' Murli kaka nodded and wandered off into the next room.

Shimplya shook his round head woefully after scanning each face in the lock-up.

'Do you children have another project at the police station?' A woman's voice startled them. 'You are the SSP Sahib's children, aren't you? Do you remember me?'

'Oh yes!' Meera smiled at Assistant Sub-Inspector Sakhi Pawar. 'Of course we remember you!' she said, glad to meet Inspector Shevre's kind deputy, who had given them a guided tour of the police station the last time they were here. 'We were just passing by and decided to step in to say hello to Inspector Shevre.'

'Oh, sir is off duty now,' sighed Sakhi Pawar. 'He left an hour ago and will be back tomorrow morning. I can give him your message if you like.'

Meera pursed her lips. Luck seemed to be on their side. 'Actually, I...uh...we...' she approached the assistant sub-inspector.

'Do you need something? Can I help you?' Sakhi Pawar stepped towards them.

'Our friend's father was called to the police station today. My friend is a little worried and I wanted to help him.'

'And who is this friend?'

'His name is Shimplya,' Meera introduced Mirchi's friend. 'His father is a fisherman and his name is Surmai Jadhav. They live in the fishing colony at Anna Nagar.'

'When did this happen?'

'Around 3 o'clock this afternoon.'

‘I was not on duty this afternoon. But I’ll try and find out. Wait here,’ she said, before disappearing into the next room.

‘I can’t see Appa anywhere,’ Shimplya’s eyes filled with tears.

‘There’s another lock-up at the back,’ said Malhar. ‘Maybe we can check there. That’s where we found Velu last time...’

‘Shevre Sahib is not on duty now,’ Constable Murli returned to give them the information they already had. ‘Shall we go?’

‘You carry on, Murli kaka,’ said Meera. ‘Our friend here has never seen a police station and wants to take a look around.’

‘It’s a police station! Not a museum!’ Constable Murli turned up his nose at the fisherboy, before dawdling off.

‘Do excuse him,’ Meera winced. ‘He is a sweet fellow.’

Shimplya said nothing.

‘Look,’ Sakhi Pawar returned. ‘You’ve come at a busy time. There are a lot of people and I have some urgent work to attend to. But I can tell you the man you are enquiring about was brought here for some case related to turtles.’

‘Turtles?’ Meera, Malhar and Mirchi exclaimed in unison.

‘Something related to poaching of sea turtles. But there is no record of any arrest in the Police Diary for the afternoon. Perhaps he was brought for questioning and has now been sent home. I don't have any more details.'

The children stared at her.

'Why don't you come back tomorrow to check? You can also meet Inspector Shevre then,' she suggested. 'Now if you will excuse me, I need to run to attend to something else,' she said, and vanished into the next room once again.

'Did you hear that, Shimplya?' said Meera. 'It seems your father was brought here in connection to some case about sea turtles. And there is no record of an arrest.'

'She said something like turtle poaching,' mumbled Malhar. 'What is that supposed to mean?'

'And she saying maybe your Appa back home,' said Mirchi, 'you go back and check.'

Shimplya stood frozen in place, eyes unblinking, face like stone.

'Shimplya!' Mirchi shook his friend by his arm. 'Shimplya!'

'Are you not happy to hear that?' asked Malhar 'Looks like he was just brought in for questioning and it's all done and over. There is no record of an arrest in the books.'

'It's not over,' Shimplya grit his teeth, mad rage in his eyes.

Meera, Malhar and Mirchi stepped back, confused by Shimplya's reaction. The boy appeared to have taken on a new persona all of a sudden—no longer sorry and pitiful, but bitter and fierce.

'It's far from being done and over!' Shimplya quivered, jaw trembling, face red, palms tightened into fists. He turned around, then stormed off in a huff. 'It's far from being done and over!'

4

Clearing the Air

'Isaac Sir!' exclaimed Meera, spotting a familiar face in the corridor outside. 'That's my photography teacher,' she told Mirchi, making her way towards a slim youth in dull denims and a white cotton shirt with a cap. 'What are you doing here, sir?'

'Meera! Well...young lady...I may as well ask you the same question!' The young man turned to her in surprise. 'What are you doing here?'

'I...uh...I'm here to help a friend make some inquiries,' she said, before introducing Malhar and Mirchi, her eyes spotting Shimplya in the distance, hurrying off towards the road leading to the beach.

'We're in the same boat then,' replied Isaac. 'I'm here to help a friend make some inquiries too,' he pointed to a young girl in a grey kurti by his side. 'You've met Akhila, haven't you?'

'Of course,' Meera nodded. 'I had joined you and Akhila for the birding photography workshop last month. You're a wildlife biologist, aren't you? And you work for an animal welfare trust, if I remember correctly.'

'Good memory,' Akhila smiled.

'Honestly, I can't make up my mind if I want to be a photographer or a biologist when I grow up,' said Meera. 'I find both fields fascinating.'

'Photographer,' winked Isaac. 'At least you won't find yourself in police stations like this.'

'Don't scare her,' Akhila admonished her friend. 'Wildlife biologists don't keep visiting police stations. This is an odd case. Don't listen to him!'

'So,' Meera said hesitantly, 'what sort of odd case would bring a wildlife biologist to a police station?'

'Well, it's a long story, but to give you the gist,' Akhila shrugged, 'the beaches around this area are a popular turtle nesting site. Thousands of turtles visit these beaches every winter to lay their eggs. But most hatchlings don't survive.'

Meera's eyes grew wide. *TURTLES*, did she say? Why was the whole world suddenly talking about turtles?

'You see, female turtles lay eggs on the beach, bury them in the sand, and swim away,' Akhila began to explain upon noticing Meera's perplexed face. 'When the eggs hatch, the babies must make their way to the sea on their own. But while some eggs and baby turtles get eaten by dogs,' she continued, 'some are hunted by humans. Many baby turtles die due to disorientation caused by street lights...they go towards land after hatching instead of walking towards the sea.'

Meera's eyebrows narrowed, unable to understand how these turtle nesting details had anything to do with being at the police station.

'These sea turtles are endangered and protected under the Wildlife Protection Laws of the country,' Akhila finally veered towards the point. 'And our trust works on turtle conservation—amongst other things. As the nesting season picks up, we assist the forest department in patrolling the beaches to keep turtles safe, and any violations are reported to the police. So, I'm here to speak to them about a case related to that.'

'You know, this might seem strange, but,' Meera beckoned Malhar and Mirchi closer. 'We know this person, a fisherman by the name of Surmai Jadhav. He was brought in here today for something to do with turtles. Do you think the two things are connected?'

'You know him?' Akhila cocked her head.

'My friend Mirchi here knows him. And my brother and I actually accompanied him here to enquire about Surmai Jadhav. Do you know anything about why he was brought here?'

'Yes,' Akhila nodded, 'And frankly, I'm here to talk to the police about the very same case.'

'Really?'

'Yes, you see, the police informed me that they'd received a tip-off about a certain fisherman suspected to be poaching sea turtles, and that they'd successfully arrested him. I was happy to hear that because I thought the authorities were finally taking the task of beach patrolling and turtle protection seriously. They also sent me a photograph of the turtles seized from this fisherman. But...' Akhila paused.

'But what?' Malhar leaned in.

'But the turtles in the picture...uh...' Akhila extracted her phone from her pocket and tapped it on to display the photos she'd received from the police.

'What about them?'

'They're not sea turtles at all!'

5

Missing Turtles

'Your father has been arrested for stealing sea turtles from the beach,' Meera gasped, finally catching up with Shimplya, who was marching off in a rage. Mirchi and Malhar got there behind her, huffing and puffing, Munna tailing along with them.

Shimplya turned around, his eyes blood red. Dismissing Meera with a flick of his hands, he walked away with big strides.

'Dekh...I know you are upset,' Mirchi took over, trotting along behind Shimplya, 'But this time, we have pukka news.'

Shimplya stopped.

'I met my photography teacher outside the police station,' explained Meera. 'His friend is a biologist working on turtle conservation. She mentioned that your father was arrested today for stealing turtles.'

'My father has nothing to do with stealing turtles!' yelled Shimplya, before turning around and stomping away to the other side of the road.

'Shimplya! Slow down!' Mirchi held up his hand to hold back traffic, following Shimplya towards the beach.

Shimplya walked on, past children building sandcastles and playing football, couples cuddling under trees, and families gathered on straw mats. In the distance, waves crashed onto the shore, beyond which, little lights shone upon ships harboured in the Maulsari bay. Above, the sky was painted in deep hues of red and purple. It all appeared idyllic and calm; all except Shimplya. The boy was bolting ahead in a rage, the M4 tailing behind him. After walking on for several minutes, Shimplya finally settled down on a rock by the water's edge.

'My Appa is not a thief! That's all I know. He is honest and hard-working,' Shimplya finally gave vent to his emotions, wiping his tears with his sleeves.

'Perhaps he accidentally harmed the turtles then?' Meera ventured a guess, balancing herself on a rock next to him.

'No, he couldn't have,' Shimplya said through a curtain of tears. 'He is the last man in Maulsari who could harm turtles.'

'Relax, dost!' Mirchi pressed Shimplya's shoulder. 'Maybe there's something you don't know and—'

'Even if harm were to come to us, Appa wouldn't harm turtles.' Shimplya rolled up the sleeve of his shirt to display a tattoo on his arm.

Scrunching up their eyes, the others peered at the figure on Shimplya's hand under the fading light of dusk.

'That's so cool,' said Malhar, his head at a tilt, 'you have a turtle tattoo!'

'The turtle is our totem. We would never harm it,' said Shimplya.

'Totem?' asked Malhar.

But Shimplya went on without pausing to explain. 'Last year when fishermen were told to stop using trawlers to prevent harming turtles, my father was one of the first to follow the advice. He even asked other fishermen to do the same. Now why would he go and steal turtles?'

'Arre...tu kya bol raha hai?' Mirchi threw up his hands. 'I can't follow a word!'

'Dekh,' Shimplya sighed, 'when we go fishing, we end up catching not just fish, but several other creatures like turtles as well. They are accidental catch. With fishermen now moving away from traditional fishing nets to large trawler boats for fishing, they end up trapping hundreds of turtles in the trawlers.'

'Hmm...' Meera nodded, 'Go on...'

'Last year, we were told by the Fisheries Department of the government that the trawlers are killing thousands of turtles and we were advised to stop using them. We wouldn't want to harm the turtles... You see, we worship them. So, my father agreed and requested other fishermen to do the same, asking them to revert to the traditional methods of fishing.'

'So, what happened then?'

'Many fishermen resisted. The trawlers are faster. The catch is larger. More fish means more money.'

'Baat toh sahi hai,' nodded Mirchi.

'My father was the first person in the fishing colony at Anna Nagar to say that we need to go back to our traditional ways of hook and net fishing even if it meant lesser profits. For the sake of the turtles and other life that was being needlessly killed. Like I said, the turtle is our totem. We wouldn't harm it for anything in the world!'

'What is this totem business?' Malhar whispered into his sister's ears.

'As his campaign found more supporters,' Shimplya continued, 'he was threatened by people who did not want to give up trawlers. Communities like ours who worship turtles are a minority. There was a lot of tension and fighting. A lot of name-calling and abusing between the two groups. My father is caught in the middle of this mess.'

'Wow,' pouted Malhar. 'I never once thought of all this while I ate fish!'

'You know,' Meera nodded thoughtfully, 'this seems to add up to what Akhila told us. It does seem like someone is trying to get your father into trouble.'

'Meaning?' Shimplya stared at Meera.

'So it seems the police claim to have caught a sack full of sea turtles from your father's boat,' Meera explained, 'But apparently they are not sea turtles at all. Akhila said they were all fresh-water turtles!'

'Really?' Shimplya's eyes grew wide. 'Are you sure?'

'Look...I don't know. But Akhila is a turtle expert. I'm sure she knows the difference. She told me that although poaching sea turtles and fresh-water turtles are both punishable crimes, it seemed odd to her that the pictures of turtles that the police sent her from the beach were of fresh-water turtles which are actually found only in inland waters.'

'But Didi, what difference does that make?' asked Malhar.

'Of course it makes a big difference!' Shimplya stood up, recharged by this piece of information. 'They produce some fresh-water turtles, claim they found it in my father's boat and accuse him of poaching them from the beach! Obviously, this means—'

'...that someone has planted them there to get your father into trouble!' Mirchi completed the sentence.

'Exactly!' Shimplya slapped one hand over the other. 'Someone who doesn't like his stand on banning turtle trawlers wants him out of the way.'

'Now...who can be doing that?' asked Mirchi.

'There are many people,' Shimplya had his gaze fixed on a ship on the horizon, 'many who have a lot at stake in this trawler business.'

'I see what you mean,' Meera nodded thoughtfully, the whole thing suddenly making sense to her for the first time that evening. 'But surely planting a sack full of fresh-water turtles is not so easy. Where would one get them from?'

'I don't know about that,' shrugged Shimplya. 'But this is surely a great lead.'

'I'll find out more from Isaac Sir and Akhila,' Meera glanced at her watch. 'It's getting late...let's meet tomorrow morning at ten at our usual place under the banyan tree in the maidan.'

'Didi, I don't follow,' said Malhar, as they waved the others goodbye and turned homeward after giving Munna a big cuddle. 'What exactly is the lead?'

'Someone is trying to get Shimplya's father into trouble,' explained Meera. 'The lead is to look out for anyone who wants Surmai Jadhav out of their way, and who can plant a sack full of turtles in his boat.'

6

Lessons over Dinner

'What's an animal protected under the schedule of the Wildlife Protection Law?' asked Meera, gulping down her soup.

Ma looked up in surprise, her eyes darting from Meera to Malhar, then back to Meera. 'What are you two up to now?' She eyed them with suspicion; and with good reason too. During the summer holidays, the children had teamed up with Mirchi and his dog Munna, to solve a neighbourhood burglary, which had resulted in unearthing a huge idol smuggling racket. Now, any question they raised about the law or police procedure, only served to make her suspicious.

'Nothing, just curious,' shrugged Meera. 'Heard this somewhere...so I wanted to know what it meant.'

'Madhavi, I'm sure these two are up to something again,' muttered Aaji, churning buttermilk in a large pot to make ghee.

'No Ma, I'm just curious,' repeated Meera. 'I met Isaac Sir's friend who is a biologist and she mentioned it in passing. So, I wanted to know. That's all.'

An experienced lawyer, Madhavi Pradhan had no difficulty in seeing through the earnest eyes and empty words of the cleverest of criminals. As she served the children more salad, she noticed they made no protest, which coupled with their exaggerated shoulder shrugs and vigorous head-shakes convinced her that it was more than a passing query. 'Alright,' she sighed. 'The Wildlife Protection Law, as the name suggests, is a law for protecting plants and animals in the wild. As you know, many animals are threatened or are on the brink of extinction. The cheetah for instance had become extinct in India.'

Meera nodded. She had read about that unfortunate event and about the recent re-introduction of cheetahs from Africa.

'So,' Ma continued, serving the children rice and dal, 'in order to ensure that this sort of thing does not happen again, the Wildlife Protection Act came into being, under which a list of endangered species was drawn up. The law has a bunch of lists—called Schedule I, Schedule II and so on. Harming, hunting, or trading in any species listed out in those Schedules is illegal.'

'So,' asked Malhar, completely absorbed, 'anyone who hunts a creature listed in those Schedules is committing a crime?'

'Arre deva!' mumbled Aaji. 'This obsession with crime seems to be a disease running in our family.'

'That's right,' nodded their mother. 'Hunting tigers, rhinos, elephants, and such other creatures named in those lists is a crime. Not only that, trading or selling any parts of these animals like elephant tusks or rhino horns or tiger skins is also a crime.'

'What about turtles?' asked Malhar. 'Is it a crime to own and sell sea turtles?'

'And what about river turtles?' added Meera. 'Are turtles endangered?'

Ma drew a deep breath. 'I know about the law, beta... not so much about turtles. But you are in luck. There's a tea party tomorrow at the Collector's home. He has invited many of us, including Baba and me. The DCF is a good friend of ours and is also going to be there. Why don't you come along tomorrow and find out all the information you want?'

'DCF?' asked Malhar.

'Deputy Conservator of Forests,' said Ma. 'Like Baba is the Senior Superintendent from the Police Service, DCF is a position in the Forest Service.'

'Perfect!' smiled Meera. 'I will join you!'

'Where are you both off to?' SSP Pradhan strode into the room.

'Baba, you're late again!' complained Malhar. 'You promised to come early and take us to the club for badminton.'

‘Sorry beta,’ SSP Pradhan ruffled his son’s curly hair. ‘It was a busy day. I promise to take you on Sunday. So, what have you been up to? First day of your Christmas holidays! Anything interesting?’

‘Very interesting,’ Ma replied on their behalf. ‘They have dozens of questions about Scheduled creatures of the wildlife law and about endangered turtles.’

‘Hmm...strange coincidence,’ SSP Pradhan tossed a slice of carrot into his mouth.

‘What coincidence?’ Meera cocked her head.

‘Last week, an international red alert was put out for the protection of sea turtles. And only yesterday, our Environment Ministry issued a circular directing all authorities to strictly enforce turtle conservation rules.’

‘What does that mean, Baba?’ Malhar scrunched his eyes.

‘That means,’ said Baba, picking up a coaster and making it spin on the table, ‘...turtle poachers better beware!’

7

A Beginning

'No,' Mirchi shook his head despondently, looking up at Malhar swinging from the roots of the banyan tree above them. 'Shimplya's father isn't back home.'

The M4 had gathered at their usual meeting spot under the massive banyan at the far end of Dhyan Chand Maidan just across the beach. A lot had changed in the six months since they'd first become friends under that very canopy. Mirchi had started going to school and conquered both the Hindi and English alphabet with help from Meera, Malhar and Paromita Ghosh, their art teacher turned ally. Meera and Malhar had turned into expert tree-climbers with regular tutorials and encouragement from Mirchi. And Munna had transformed from a scraggy mongrel into a fat fluffy ball, now that he was fed three times what he ate earlier.

'Isaac Sir promised to find out more from Akhila and tell me,' said Meera, pulling out the M4 badges she'd made them all, after they'd first teamed up. 'I have to call him back in the afternoon.'

'So...' Malhar jumped down with a thud, 'what do we do now?'

'Look,' Meera flipped open a diary she'd begun for this case and went over the points she'd noted. 'Shimplya says his father couldn't have harmed turtles. And from what he told us about that turtle totem and his father's fight to stop trawlers, it does seem like someone is trying to get him into trouble.'

'But Didi, the police must have had some reason for arresting him, na?' Malhar held out a packet of chewing gum before Mirchi. 'Remember Baba told us about some red alert for turtle smuggling?'

'What reason Inspector Shevre having, for arresting Velu last time?' Mirchi reminded Malhar of the police excesses they had witnessed during their first case.

'By the way, what is this totem business?' asked Malhar, pinning his M4 badge upon his black t-shirt that sported an array of avengers.

'I read about it last night,' said Meera, tapping a note she'd scribbled at the back of her blue diary. 'It is an animal that a tribe considers sacred. It could be a horse, a parrot, a turtle—any creature that is special for the tribe. It becomes their symbol. People of that tribe worship it and do not kill or eat that animal as a mark of respect.'

'So,' Malhar held a ball before Munna then flung it across the grass, 'the turtle being the totem for these fishermen means that they will not harm or eat them.'

'More reason to trust Shimplya's father's side of the story,' nodded Meera.

'I knowing Shimplya father,' said Mirchi, as Munna came bounding towards him with the ball in his mouth. 'He good man.'

'If he is innocent, we need to find out who planted the turtles in his boat,' said Meera. 'That is the only way we can help Shimplya's dad.'

'See, I knowing one snakecharmer in Anand Nagar,' suggested Mirchi. 'His name Shambhu Nath. He also arrested one time, not for turtle but for snake. We can ask him what happened in his case. And there is one other fellow—Murtuza bhai.' Mirchi threw the ball again into the distance as Munna ran back to fetch it. 'He selling pet animals—birds, fish—I hearing he having turtles also. We can go to his shop.'

'How will that help?' Malhar plonked on the grass and opened a box of chaklis.

'If someone putting turtles in Shimplya father boat, we needing to know who can be giving such big supply. Murtuza bhai having pet shop so he knowing turtle suppliers,' Mirchi munched on a chakli. 'He having one small shop in Anand Nagar and big shop at Domed Market. We can go and ask, na.'

'Why not?' Meera nodded. 'There can't be too many people in Maulsari selling turtles.'

'Exactly!' Mirchi snapped his fingers. 'Who knowing? Murtuza bhai supplier may be supplier of person who putting turtles in Shimplya father boat!'

'I think we're going at a complete tangent,' Malhar clicked his teeth. 'It's a waste of time.'

'We don't have much to do until the Collector's tea party anyway, so let's go!' Meera returned her pencil and diary into the bag and stood up. 'And besides, we have nowhere else to start. Forget the snakecharmer, let's go to the pet store and check.'

'But don't go there and start asking questions,' warned Mirchi as they made their way across to the other end of the maidan. 'Murtuza bhai getting suspicious. You act like you wanting to buy pets. Then he talking to you.'

'Alright! Let's pretend,' smiled Malhar. 'That's the best part about being a detective anyway!' He rubbed his palms, eager to have another chance to tread in the shoes of Fatty of the Five Find-Outers who solved mysteries during their holidays, often dressing up in curious disguises.

Crossing the road, the M4 turned into Anand Nagar, the basti where six months ago their nascent detective dreams had taken root with Meera and Malhar following Mirchi and Munna into the narrow by-lanes, like strangers in their own city. But today, they walked without staring at the tin-topped structures and dingy little rooms; even smiling and nodding at some familiar faces.

'Where is this Murtuza bhai's shop? asked Malhar, now familiar with large areas of this sprawling cluster.

'Behind that poster,' Mirchi pointed to a gaudy billboard where an array of beaming politicians were dousing their party leader in a shower of flowers, wishing him a glorious future on the occasion of his ninetieth birthday. 'I telling that you both are customers.'

'You let me do the talking,' Meera told her brother. 'If you open your big mouth, that will be the end of our investigation.'

'Yeah right!' snapped Malhar, as they came upon an open ground where feral pigs huddled around a pile of garbage. 'You remember the last time we went undercover? You were caught out. I dressed as a beggar and got away.'

'Arre bhai, stop arguing,' Mirchi turned about. 'And get those badges off! Munna, you waiting here for us near tanki.' He pointed to the huge water tank, as Munna dropped his wagging tail, let out a little whine, and deposited himself reluctantly in the shade. 'And haan...' Mirchi's voice dropped to a hushed whisper as they reached a door with beaded curtains at the head of the next alley. 'Whatever you saying, don't tell you are SSP Sahib's bacha-log, else Murtuza bhai skinning me alive!'

8

Endangered

Mirchi knocked on the wooden door. No answer. He knocked again.

'Who is it?' a gruff voice came from inside.

'Arre main...Mirchi.'

'What do you want?'

'I have brought customers.'

Silence.

'Are you coming or what?' Mirchi exchanged glances with the siblings.

No response.

'They want to buy some birds.'

Again, no response.

'Okay then,' Mirchi winked, 'If you're busy, I'll take them to Salim bhai's pet shop at Khan Market.'

The door creaked open.

'Business doesn't begin so early!' A lean young man with a pock-marked face dressed in a sleeveless vest and blue jeans emerged, phone in one hand, bunch of keys in the other.

'Junaid!' smiled Mirchi. 'Is Murtuza bhai not home?'

Junaid didn't care to answer. 'What kind of birds do you want?' He glared at Mirchi, then looked Meera and Malhar up and down, gauging their purchase power from their clothes, shoes, and watches.

'Uh...ah...' Malhar mumbled, certain that his grandmother would have taken one look at the fellow's face and called him *suran* or elephant yam!

Uncomfortable with Junaid's gaze, Meera pulled her navy blue shrug over her t-shirt. 'A pair of love-birds,' she said.

'That would be two thousand rupees each.'

'Can we see them first?' asked Malhar.

Junaid fumbled with the keys, then opened a little door on his right and motioned for the kids to step in.

Ducking through the low doorframe, Mirchi, Meera and Malhar entered a dimly lit narrow room. As their eyes adjusted to the darkness, a row of cages covered in a white sheet came into view. Junaid pulled off the cover, rattled a cage or two, then switched on a tube light. Suddenly dozens of creatures began to chirp and squeak and squall and quack.

Stunned, the children stared in horror at the scene before them. Cages, rows and rows of them, were stacked up from floor to ceiling. Birds chirruped from here; little white mice with pink limbs scurried about there; hamsters peeped out from some; brown Persian cats purred from others, as they swirled about to find more cages in a niche behind the door. There were fish of every size and colour in little aquarium boxes and thumb-sized turtles in transparent rectangular tubs on the floor. Feathers and animal food littered the floor of the enclosure and the air was filled with the stench of poop and grub.

Malhar had an unbearable urge to throw up, retching at the sight of animals stored like sacks of grain. They had neither air to breathe, nor space to move.

Meera wished she could open the cages and let them all free. But she managed to contain her shock, and find a feeble voice. 'You have cockatoos?' she asked Junaid, staring at the exotic birds.

'I can get you anything you want,' boasted Junaid, twirling the phone about in his hand.

'But cockatoos are not found in India...how do you get them?' Meera began probing Junaid for his sources.

'I told you,' Junaid repeated, playing with the gold chain on his neck, 'I can get you anything you want.'

'What about turtles?' asked Malhar. 'Can we get those turtles?'

'They aren't my relatives to be living with us!' Junaid guffawed, before turning his eyes to the tub. 'Ah! This one seems dead,' he said, pulling out a turtle from the water and tossing it into a plastic bin in the corner. 'Naturally they're for sale too, you joker!'

Malhar winced, unable to breath. Meera stared at the turtle lying still in the bin.

'So, you wanted love-birds, right?' Junaid continued casually, as if he'd binned no more than a piece of paper. 'Come over here.' He led them to a section at the end of the room.

'Are these sea turtles?' Meera's voice trembled, as she tore her eyes away from the dead turtle.

Junaid shook his head. 'River turtles,' he replied. 'Now you people want turtles or love-birds?'

'But where do you get river turtles from?' Meera persisted, eager to get the information and get the hell out of this wretched place.

'Love-birds,' Junaid tapped two cages with little yellow and green birds, not caring to reply. 'Which ones do you want?'

'Where do you get your stuff from?' Malhar supported his sister's earnest queries.

'That is none of your business,' Junaid fixed Malhar with a fierce stare. 'You tell me what you want.'

'I was wondering,' Meera changed tack. 'If you can get us many baby turtles. My mother might be interested in getting a bunch to give away as gifts at our new year party next week. I would also love to have some at the pond in our Bhivpur farmhouse.'

Junaid raised his eyebrows, his eyes darting from Meera's shoes to Malhar's watch. Caged birds were one thing, but turtles cost a lot of money. Before revealing any more, he had to make sure his customers were capable of paying up.

'That Salim bhai's shop you mentioned at the Khan Market,' said Meera, pulling out the clever card Mirchi had played earlier. 'Perhaps we can go there.'

'Wait!' Junaid put his phone into his pocket. A customer with a farmhouse in Bhivpur was not one to lose. 'I can get you all the turtles you want for your farmhouse and new year party gifts. But they will cost a lot of money.'

'That's not a problem,' said Meera. 'My mother wants to have the most unique gifts to give the guests. If you can be sure of arranging them, I will bring her here tomorrow.'

Mirchi stared at Meera curiously as she spun her fantastic story. Malhar scratched his head, unable to fathom how his sister was going to show up the next day with their mother, who would undoubtedly refuse to play a part in this operation.

'Bring them all to our big shop at Domed Market tomorrow,' Junaid instructed Mirchi. 'You can see what we have there, and decide what you want.'

'Zaroor bhai,' nodded Mirchi, still perplexed about how Meera planned to pull this off. 'And don't forget my commission, bhai!' he grinned, adding an authentic touch to the act. 'Give my salaam to Murtuza bhai.' He waved cheerfully to Junaid and lead the siblings through the door.

Relieved to be out, Malhar inhaled deeply. Suddenly, even the foul-smelling air by the filthy nallah of Anand

Nagar felt like a field of daisies. Meera shut her eyes, overcome by a wave of sadness, then deep anger, as Mirchi got busy calculating the money Murtuza bhai would be making selling pets. 'You don't realize your worth, Munna!' he laughed, throwing his arms around the black dog who was wagging his tail in delight. 'You animals are such big business!'

9

Tea Party

'So wonderful to meet you,' Vanaja Narula, Deputy Conservator of Forests, extended her hand to Meera and Malhar.

Meera's jaw dropped. Malhar stared at the diminutive woman with short hair. For some reason, they'd both assumed that the forest officer they were to meet would be a man.

'They're here specially to meet you,' smiled Mrs Pradhan. 'They have a lot of questions about wildlife protection and as I was seeing you today, I suggested they come along and hear all about it from you. And my mother-in-law was eager to hear all about it too.'

'I'm so glad,' Vanaja Narula smiled. 'I generally avoid these parties and dinner invitations as they bore me to death,' she whispered. 'But I couldn't wriggle out of this one, so I'm happy to find someone interested to talk about wildlife.'

'That's good, because I was feeling guilty about imposing them upon you like this,' smiled Mrs Pradhan, wrapping her beige dupatta around her arms.

'Not at all,' Vanaja Narula settled down at a low table with a cup of tea. 'I would rather talk to children about wildlife than discuss politics with bureaucrats. Besides, I've had an agonisingly exhausting week so speaking to children is a welcome break.'

'Really?' asked Mrs Pradhan. 'I imagine you living in a sylvan forest lodge waking up to birdsong and babbling brooks, as far removed as can be from agonising and exhausting.'

'That's a popular misconception,' laughed Vanaja. 'Most forest officers live in the district headquarters, not inside forests. But I spend much of my time inside, yes. It's one of the many perks of the service. But unfortunately, I seldom have the time to just sit down and enjoy it at leisure. And this week has been unusually busy.'

'So what does an exhausting week for a forest officer look like?' asked Mrs Pradhan, as Aaji leaned in to listen.

'Well, let's see,' Vanaja adjusted her saree and crossed right leg over left knee, 'the week began with supervising a teak auction, then an emergency call to save an orphaned leopard cub. And then two cases of sudden night patrolling after tip-offs we received about illegal timber felling. Some beat inspections and field visits as always, and there's been continuous pressure to approve an application for letting go of some forest land under my jurisdiction for a highway expansion project. And then some trouble with encroachers at the periphery of the jungle who turned violent and broke some forest department equipment and burnt our vehicles! So yes, it's been an eventful and hectic week,' she sighed.

All ears, Meera exchanged an excited glance with her grandmother. Saving a stranded leopard cub and night patrolling in the jungle. This sounded like the job of her dreams! She pulled up a chair.

'So, tell me,' Vanaja turned to the children. 'What is it that you want to know?'

Meera had an admiring grin pasted on her face, already growing fond of the Deputy Conservator in charge of over 10,000 acres of forest that formed the Duala National Park at the outskirts of Maulsari. 'I...I...' she hesitated. 'I often go birdwatching and love bird photography.'

'That's fantastic!' smiled Vanaja. 'I see you have a lovely pair of hornbills painted on your t-shirt. Do you have a birding group?'

'Yes, I am part of the Junior Maulsari Birding Club. I go with them.'

'Ah...with Isaac?'

'Oh yes! You know him?'

'Very well. He works closely with an NGO that often helps the Forest Department.'

'That's great, I too want to grow up and do something like that. I recently heard about a shop that sells pets. It has all kinds of birds, some Indian and some exotic. It also has many other animals like hamsters and...'

'...and turtles,' Malhar steered the conversation towards their purpose.

'The thought of all these creatures stuffed in little cages made me very uncomfortable. I was wondering if anything can be done,' Meera cracked her knuckles.

'I'm so glad to hear that you feel for these caged creatures,' began Vanaja Narula, putting down her cup of tea. 'That is refreshing because many people these days think it is okay to put animals in cages and keep them as pets at home. It is a source of entertainment—something to decorate their homes with.'

'So,' Malhar interjected. 'Is it not okay to keep these animals as pets? I mean, is it illegal?'

'Absolutely! Birds are meant to fly! Not be in cages to please people. To keep birds in cages as pets at home is against the law.'

'But there are so many of these birds there...love-birds and cockatoos.'

'These are exotic birds,' said Vanaja Narula. 'Because it is illegal to cage and sell wild Indian birds, these guys get birds from outside India, which are not covered under the Indian law. These love-birds and exotic parrots are all caught in African and East Asian jungles, stuffed into bags and boxes and shipped illegally to pet markets around the world. The tragedy is,' she continued, 'even if you save them and free them, they wouldn't be able to survive on their own because they have always lived in captivity.'

'And uh...what about turtles?' Malhar pointed to the smiling Ninja turtle on his green t-shirt.

'Well, there are several species of turtles,' said Vanaja, sitting back in her chair. 'And a large number of them are endangered, vulnerable or threatened and hence protected under the Wildlife Protection Law. So yes, it is illegal to hunt and trade in turtles too.'

The thought of Junaid carelessly flicking a turtle into a bin sent a shiver up Meera's spine.

'But why do so many people want to buy turtles and other creatures? Just to keep them as pets at home?' asked Aaji, pulled into the conversation.

'That's a good question, and frankly, the answer fits into a very wide range,' replied the DCF. 'Turtle soup is a delicacy in some parts of the world. The Chinese make medicine out of tiger bones and wine out of pangolin blood. And then there are all kinds of other things. Organs of monitor lizards are used for tantric rituals to attract young girls! The scales of pangolins are used to make drugs! The extent and scale of this thing is just mindnumbing.'

'Lizard body parts for tantric rituals to attract girls?' Mrs Pradhan put down her tea cup, completely horrorstruck.

'Scoundrels!' muttered Aaji. 'Back in my village a holy man once sacrificed a young girl because he had a dream that it would help him find buried treasure! Rotten people! Brinjal-heads! They can do anything!'

'Absolutely,' agreed the DCF. 'Many people believe turtles and sand boas are signs of good luck and prosperity. Tiger and leopard skin make for trophies on the walls of the wealthy and powerful. Some people are willing to pay a fortune for bracelets made of rhino horn and jewellery made of elephant tusks and trinkets made of turtle shell and what not! It doesn't matter to them that it involves the butchering of wildlife. Its mindless!'

'Do people not know, what buying these items involves?' Mrs Pradhan put down her cup and leaned forward, perplexed by all that she'd been hearing. 'I thought there is rising awareness these days about topics like climate change and sustainability.'

'Nearly 50,000 elephants are massacred for their tusks each year but do you know what a survey conducted in China found? Most people did not know that ivory came from elephants! And still others thought the elephants just dropped their tusks and grew new ones like a snake's skin. They had no idea it involved the massacre of elephants! So a lot of it has to do with zero awareness. And as it turns out, much of our poached wildlife—from tiger skins to elephant tusks and more—

are smuggled to China, Myanmar, Vietnam, Thailand. It is a big big business.'

Nearly every word Vanaja Narula had said bolstered Meera's resolve to turn into a wildlife warrior and set free all the helpless creatures she'd seen that morning.

'It gets worse,' Vanaja Narula continued, waving casually to an acquaintance in the distance. 'The wildlife trade is closely linked with the gun and drug mafia. The money made from trading in illegal wildlife goes into buying weapons and running drug cartels. It's a highly clandestine nexus involving dangerous power games. What many people don't understand when they buy these kinds of things is that not only are they participating in decimating wildlife, but also unwittingly bankrolling wealthy drug lords, powerful politicians, and notorious gangsters that operate behind a masked front.'

'So a large part of your work must involve tracking down these poachers,' said Mrs Pradhan, as eager now as the children to understand this phenomenon.

'Often we are able to nab the hunter and almost always, they're poor villagers at the forest periphery with no other source of livelihood. Or we are able to trace the local trader. But these are the small fish that get trapped in the crossfire. The real challenge is to get to the kingpin, the link between the source in our jungles, and the international customers. In fact, we know for some years now that a poaching racket has been on in the Daula National Park, and the wildlife is transported out through Maulsari. But we haven't been able to catch the kingpin.'

'But these poor people who are hunting the animals in the jungles,' said Aaji, 'if they're given other jobs, perhaps they'd stop hunting and the whole thing can be brought to an end?'

Vanaja Narula exhaled hard. 'I wish things were as simple, but it's a very complicated problem. You see, perceptions of wildlife are different for different people, depending on where you come from. To city people, wildlife is gorgeous tigers and majestic elephants—precious animals to be protected, so that they may gaze at them on safaris during their holidays. But those who live in close proximity to the forest have a very different lived experience.'

'Meaning?' asked Malhar. 'They don't value these animals like city people?'

'On the contrary,' smiled the DCF. 'The tribals have a very close relation with the forest and value it and love it in ways that we cannot begin to understand. The forest is divine for them, and they worship predators like tigers and leopards as their gods.'

Meera nodded, recalling Shimplya's turtle totem. 'Then why do they hunt them?'

'You see, for centuries these people have lived in the forest when hunting was a way of life. Earlier, rajas, nawabs, and the British valued them for their sharp hunting and trapping skills. Then the Indian wildlife law was passed in 1972, and their occupations became illegal. Many of these people who'd been completely dependent on the forest for hunting or wood cutting or animal grazing or collection of small forest produce like tendu leaves for bidis, mahua flowers for liquor and so on, found their way of life outlawed.'

Meera turned to her mother. She'd always thought about the law as something that protected people, as a tool for justice. It never occurred to her that the law could unfairly disadvantage people so.

'So due to our laws, these people find themselves forcibly removed and resettled often in land which is fallow and unproductive, as the government slowly took over control of forests for Project Tiger, Project Elephant and so on. They often have no choice except to go back to the forest and return to the occupations for which they have skills.'

'But these projects were essential, weren't they? To save the tiger...else it would have become extinct like the cheetah.'

Vanaja smiled again. 'That is why I began by saying it's a very complicated problem. It's not black and white, but a whole lot of grey.'

Overwhelmed and dejected, Meera exchanged a glance with Malhar. While they'd started out to help Shimplya's father, it appeared like they were now staring at a much bigger problem. And if for decades the police and Forest Department had not been able to crack the case with all the experience, manpower and resources at their disposal, what chance did the M4 have?

10

Dirty Games

The squat man in the brown safari suit adjusted the designer sunglasses over his plump face and gazed out from the podium at the vast crowd gathered at the beach.

'It is now as clear as day,' he hollered into the microphone, 'on the one hand, these people want trawlers taken off on the pretext of protecting turtles. Then under cover of darkness, they slyly steal turtles and sell them at exorbitant prices. But now the dirty game is over! No more! No more! We say no more!'

A round of roars and cheers followed.

'Who is this man?' whispered Meera.

'Keshav Rathi,' Shimplya spat in contempt, ready to charge towards the stage and pummel the speaker. 'He is the local thug turned politician. He started with nothing. And today, he lives in a palatial bungalow on that fancy Palm Beach Road. He owns a large fisheries business which packages and exports frozen seafood to big hotels and foreign customers. He also gets a hefty commission from Chinese companies selling trawlers here.'

'What about all these people?' asked Meera, looking around at the vast crowds. 'Do they all support him?'

'Not everyone, but many do,' said Shimplya, looking on as a group of fishermen stepped forward on the dais to garland Rathi, thanking him profusely for helping them in times of trouble. Rathi edged one of them towards the mike, encouraging him to say a few words.

'I...uh..' the fisherman dabbed his teary eyes, 'for ten months we had been rotting in a jail in Pakistan. Our fault? We had unknowingly strayed into Pakistani waters. And...and...uh nobody cared about us. Thanks to Rathi sahib for his help we are back home now, united with our families.' He raised Rathi's hand up. 'Keshav Rathi Saheb ki...' he yelled into the microphone.

'Jai!'

'Keshav Rathi Saheb ki...'

'Jai!'

The air resounded with cries and cheers, as a row of fishermen and their families stepped forward, to bury Rathi in garlands before falling at his feet.

'He seems like a really popular man,' Mirchi crossed his hands across his chest.

Shimplya swallowed hard. 'During bad times, even those you trust, desert you.' He cast a despondent eye at those around. 'Except a handful in my community, all these people—they're drawn to this snake!'

'It is time now to unite, my friends!' Keshav Rathi handed his garlands to his bodyguard and grabbed the mike once again. 'To expose these hypocrites who say one thing by day and do another at night. Like I have brought our fellow fishermen back from Pakistani jails, I shall be by your side through every hazard and hardship. Place your faith in me, dear friends and I assure you that together we shall build a promising future for us all!'

Claps. Whistles. Cheers.

'Look at that bodyguard,' snickered Malhar, pointing to the beefy man behind Rathi. 'He has such an enormous moustache.'

'He's Muchhad. Rathi's henchman,' said Shimplya. 'He does all of Rathi's dirty work.'

'Dirty work?'

'Demanding hafta, threatening people, beating those who don't listen. He tried to get Appa to back off from this anti-trawler campaign by sending him all sorts of threats. All this helping poor fisherman is just a farce... All he did was to write a letter to someone. The real work was done by a kind man who runs a group that routinely helps fishermen stranded in Pakistani waters. It happens very often. This Rathi is just milking this case to gain popularity, as he wants to stand for elections next year.'

'Hey, wait a minute!' Mirchi's eyes grew wide. 'Rathi opposing your father, Rathi threatening him in the past, Rathi having money to buy many turtles!'

Shimplya nodded slightly. 'Yes, some of the elders in my community suspect that Rathi may be playing a dirty game with Appa. He is loaded. He can buy all the turtles in the world if he wanted to. But there's no proof. And he's so powerful who will listen to us...' his voice trailed off.

'If Rathi wants your father out of the way so fishermen can continue using his Chinese trawlers, what better than make use of this red alert to get him arrested?' Meera nodded, seeing merit in Mirchi's theory.

'And if he has the reach and power to get fisherman out of jails in Pakistan, how difficult could it be for such a man to plant some turtles and money on a boat right here in Maulsari?' added Malhar.

'Maybe we should probe this angle,' Meera bit her nails, the chat with Vanaja Narula flashing before her. *Mafia. Money. Illegal. Clandestine. Power-games.* The words and expressions she'd heard earlier that day seemed to float in like pieces of a jigsaw puzzle. *Politicians. Nexus. Poor at the crossroads. Masked front.* Was Shimplya's father just a poor person caught at the crossroads of a clandestine operation? She was reminded of Velu, the plumber wrongly accused of a burglary in the last case they'd solved together. His plight, more than anything, had spurred their investigation on. This time, perhaps, it was to be a poor fisherman's predicament. 'Mirchi, I think you're right. We should check about this Rathi,' she said.

Standing astride over Munna, Mirchi rubbed his soft ears, thinking about how he could get more information on this man.

'And we should also continue to follow up with Junaid for those turtles. Hopefully that will lead us to his network,' added Meera.

'And I need to find a lawyer,' Shimplya clicked his tongue.

'Hey,' Malhar turned to him. 'My mother is a lawyer. I'm sure she can help you! We'll go back and speak to her right away. Why don't you come to her office tomorrow afternoon?'

Shimplya sighed, his face breaking into a hint of a smile for the first time in two days. As dusk gave way to twilight, he looked up at the stars slowly filling the eastern sky. Long battles lay ahead. But with the M4 by his side, hope was still afloat.

11

India of Snakecharmers

'Raid. Fine. Jail.' Seated on his haunches under the single bulb in the room, Shambhu Nath slapped his forehead with his palm. 'That is what our life has been reduced to.'

Mirchi stared at the old man, whose face was a patchwork of spots and wrinkles, his dhoti worn out and faded. Meera and Malhar had filled him in yesterday after their chat with the DCF, but he was here at the snakecharmer's house, curious to know the other side. As his wise Dadi often said, ameer-log have their view of things, and the garib-log had theirs. A good investigator simply had to know both sides.

'Beta, we sapheras or snakecharmers, are the descendants of Guru Gorakhnath, an avatar of Lord Bholenath himself,' said the bearded man, turning to an ash-smeared picture of Shiva in a little niche by the window. 'But today my been and my basket,' he tapped on his flute made of bitter-gourd that lay under the bed, 'they both lie unused and still.'

'Kaka...' Mirchi probed on. 'Weren't you once arrested for some wildlife lafda?'

The old man nodded. 'Since the time I was a small boy, I had followed my father, performing with snakes at street corners, as my forefathers had done. After the performance, we would hand out jadi-bootis and herbal medicines which we made from plants in the jungle. Often, we'd get called to help villagers catch snakes that had entered their homes. Many called us for help when someone in their family got bitten by a snake, because only we knew which snakes were venomous, and which were not and gave people antidotes for the bite. People welcomed us and respected us. In fact, so many foreigners used to flock to see our show. Some of them told me that people all over the world know India as the land of snakes and snakecharmers...' He began to cough.

'What happened then?' Mirchi poured out a glass of water from a jug and handed it to him.

'One fine morning, as I was performing just like any other day on a street, a policeman arrested me,' he continued. 'Why are you arresting me, I screamed. But that fellow told me about some blessed wildlife kanoon. He said if I trapped snakes or made them perform, I would be put in jail. Now you tell me, what is a man like me to do? This is all I know!' he rued. 'But today's world values you if understand computers, not cobras!'

'Hmm...' Mirchi nodded sympathetically, his eyes turning to the sleeping man who'd begun stirring on the straw mat by the window.

'Ask him,' said Shambhu Nath, pointing to the sunburnt bleary-eyed man. 'He is my son-in-law. His family...they all live in the Daula Forest. Ten years ago, the government recognized the rights of forest dwellers under some new law. And this poor fellow has been running from pillar to post to get one patta—a piece of paper—to show for it. But the procedures just never end! Tell him...'

The man sat up, rubbed his eyes, then nodded. 'We people don't fear the tiger,' he sighed, 'as much we fear the Forest Department.'

'Sarkari babus!' Shambu Nath clicked his tongue, folding his hands before his face and raising them above his head. 'Don't know what we have done in our past life to invite their wrath.'

'Last year they caught me taking two pots of honey from the forest and filed a case against me,' the younger man stood up, rolled his mat, and placed it against the wall. 'Now tell me, what is wrong with that?' he said, sitting cross-legged beside Mirchi. 'My baap-dada have been doing that for centuries. How am I to feed my children if they don't allow me into the jungle? And all these city people who buy honey...tell me, do they think it just falls from the sky?'

'Kaka,' Mirchi turned to Shambhu Nath to keep the conversation focused. 'You know Surmai Jadhav?'

Adjusting his red turban, the old man shook his head.

'He is a fisherman. He has also been arrested for breaking some wildlife kanoon...but he has not done anything wrong.'

'Arre beta, all these powerful people make rules as they please. They will hack down jungles to build roads, factories and farmhouses; destroy forests for mines, pollute the world with their big cars and bigger jets. But when we poor people do anything—catch a fish, hunt a boar, cut a tree, even pluck a flower—they will jump at our throats, come hollering at us! You are destroying wildlife; you are wiping out forests, they'll say.'

'Every big problem today,' the son-in-law took over, 'pollution, plastic, global warming—tell me, have they been created by us tribal people? Or these bade-log? And still, they have the authority to tell me that my honey collection is destroying the jungle!'

'Sadly, that is the way of the world,' the old man shook his head despondently. 'Power determines right and wrong. Only power matters.'

With a sigh, Mirchi tried steering the conversation back. 'So what did you do when you were arrested, bhaiya? How did you get out? How can Jadhav get out?'

'Power, Mirchi beta,' the old man repeated, 'power! If powerful people get us into trouble, only they can get us out. I was lucky. My herbs had cured a politician's son of a serious ailment once. That man was grateful to me and helped me in return and I was able to get out of jail. That's just how things work in our country. So find someone in power, and get close. That is the only ladder to escape our miserable fate—proximity to power!'

12

Murky Market

Domed Market got its name from the enormous dome that sat atop the colonial structure that was once a spice warehouse. Flanking Paromita Ghosh outside Junaid's pet shop at Domed Market, Malhar and Meera were relieved to find that the store had a window and led their art-teacher-turned-temporary-mother inside. She had been a huge support to them during the previous case they'd solved. As a die-hard fan of detective Byomkesh Bakshi, Paromita Ghosh had been only too pleased to join them in snooping around, fulfilling her childhood dream of becoming a detective.

'Turtle party,' Junaid greeted them in a dazzling red shirt. 'Please sit,' he offered Mrs Ghosh a stool, after wiping it with a cloth.

'I'm in a bit of a hurry,' Mrs Ghosh placed her sunglasses over her head and turned down the seat. 'Please tell me about the turtles.'

'Great gift idea you having, madam. How many you needing? We provide you with everything. Please have seat, madam,' Junaid said deferentially, his arrogant persona completely transformed at the sight of the well-dressed lady adorned with gold bangles and diamond earrings.

'Look, I told you I'm in a hurry. I just want to know—'

'We...uh...we providing whatever you need, madam,' Junaid shifted on his feet. 'Look, this red-eared slider... this size,' he pulled out an album with laminated photographs and held up his palm. 'And this,' he flipped the page, 'This Indian star tortoise, very popular pet. Lot of people buying. And this...'

'What's all this?' Mrs Ghosh flared her nostrils. 'I'm not here to see pictures! You told my children you'll be showing us the turtles at the shop.'

'Madam madam,' Junaid's eyes darted to the road outside. 'I arranging whatever you want madam but you see,' he whispered, 'police troubling us if they seeing turtles here. So we first taking order and taking advance from the customer. Then we delivering direct to them.'

'Look here,' Mrs Ghosh said sternly, 'I leave for the farmhouse in two days and after my children mentioned turtles yesterday, I have promised my husband to stun our New Year guests with unusual return gifts. We just don't do ordinary gifts like middle-class people,' she flicked her hair. 'I am an established Feng Shui master and turtles are said to bring good luck. I simply must have them. Don't give me all this nonsense about order and advance. You think I can't pay? Just tell me where you get them from and we'll arrange to go right away.'

Malhar pursed his lips to suppress a smile, marvelling at his art teacher's acting abilities.

'Madam, I promise, madam,' Junaid assured his esteemed customer. 'You will have the turtles. But—'

A noisy scooter spluttered to a halt outside the shop, then its orange-haired rider stepped inside with an authoritative air. If Junaid had the eyes of a hawk, this man was an x-ray scanner. His deep-set eyes bore into Mrs Ghosh first, then the two children, deducing within seconds their purchase power and societal status.

'Abba,' Junaid turned to the older man in a brown kurta, eager to convey that he had acquired a big client. 'This party wants turtles...large order. Urgent hai.'

So this was Murtuza bhai, thought Meera, remembering Mirchi's advice. *The son is a bit of a buffoon, but don't mess with the father!*

Pulling up a steel stool, Murtuza bhai plonked himself in front of a table fan. 'Turtles?' he asked through paan-stained teeth. 'What kind of turtles?'

'Fresh-water turtles,' replied Meera.

'Yesterday this boy told my children that we could come to your shop and get the turtles,' said Mrs Ghosh.

'You see, madam,' Junaid explained, 'Trading in these turtles is not legal, so we not keeping them openly at shop.'

'Ah...is that so?' Mrs Ghosh feigned surprise, as if it were news for her.

'But we can get them for you,' Junaid smiled. 'We have sources.'

'It will cost you 5000 per piece,' said Murtuza bhai, drumming his fingers on the counter. 'Fifty per cent advance.'

Mrs Ghosh waved off the remark as if the price didn't pinch her, then pulled out her mobile. 'Hello Rewa jaan,' she spoke loudly into her mobile. 'I'm so sorry I can't join you in Greece. I have to attend my nephew's wedding in London next month.'

Murtuza bhai's ears pricked up, his eyes scanning every garment and accessory on Mrs Ghosh, even as Meera and Malhar exchanged admiring glances, blown away by their art teacher's performance.

Aware that she had the man's full attention, the pretend-mom went on. 'Yes, I'm so sorry darling. I feel terrible about missing your anniversary. Have a wonderful cruise, you all. Give my love to the children... and we'll meet in New York next summer. Ciao my love, mmmuah mmmuah,' she blew kisses at her device, then hung up. 'Alright then,' she turned to the children. 'Come, you mentioned some other pet shop perhaps we should try there. I'm sure they'll be more reasonable.'

'What is the hurry, madam?' Murtuza bhai smiled, unwilling to let go of a wealthy client. 'The price is secondary. Customer satisfaction is more important.

You take a look first, madam. We can always discuss the price later.'

'You may be a clever businessman,' remarked Mrs Ghosh, 'but I am not a fool! Besides, I don't have time to waste. I leave for my farmhouse in two days where we have a grand New Year bash planned. The wealthiest industrialists are going to be present—my husband's business associates from Dubai and Hong Kong,' Mrs Ghosh was enjoying herself thoroughly now.

'In that case madam, perhaps I can show you something more exotic and extraordinary than turtles?'

'What do you mean?'

'Imagine your wealthy industrialist friends from Dubai enter your farmhouse...' Murtuza bhai transformed into a storyteller. 'And imagine the walls of your living room decorated with tiger skins, rhino horns and elephant tusks. Now wouldn't that impress them?'

Speechless, Meera stared at the man. 'Do you kill these tigers or use their skin after they are dead?' asked Malhar.

'Arre chote nawab,' Murtuza bhai ruffled the boy's thick hair. 'You're too young to know these gory details.'

'No,' Mrs Ghosh said stoically, her face taking on a ghostly pallor. Growing up in West Bengal, she'd visited the Sundarbans—the beautiful forest—where the majestic Bengal tiger was not just a predator, but also a god. The thought that this man could speak so casually about hanging up their skins as curios, shook her to the bone. 'I would like to know too,' she said, trying to pass off anger as curiosity. 'How do you procure these skins and horns?'

'Oh madam, why bother your good-self with all this? Leave that to us!' he laughed. 'Can I offer you some tea, coffee or nasta?' his conversation sailed from tiger skins to tea as if it were a matter of course.

'Well, hmm,' Mrs Ghosh shifted uneasily on her feet, trying her best to stay in character. 'I...would have to check with my husband, although I suspect he would quite like the idea of having a trophy in the living room of our farmhouse. It would command awe, nai?'

'Indeed madam,' Murtuza bhai nodded, fishing out his visiting card from his pocket. 'Please contact me for anything you or your friends need.'

'For now,' Mrs Ghosh supressed the urge to throw the card back on the man's face, 'I'd be happy to know more about the turtles,' she said, quickly masking her discomfort. 'We want a large number so I assume you will be reasonable with the price.'

'You have my word,' Murtuza bhai held his ears with his fingers to convey his promise, then signalled to Junaid to get on a call with someone. 'You will be going back to your farmhouse with the turtles in two days and present your guests with the most extraordinary of gifts.'

'I can't get through,' whispered Junaid.

Whacking his son on his head, Murtuza bhai grabbed the phone from his hand and dialled the number himself. Unable to connect, he tried again.

'I told you I cannot reach them,' Junaid whined. 'The signal there is really poor.'

'Then you must go there right away,' said the father. 'Don't you understand the customer is in a hurry?'

'Tch...' Junaid took back his phone and tried again.

'Madam, please leave your phone number with me,' said Murtuza bhai. 'I will call you as soon as I have the maal.'

'No,' replied Mrs Ghosh sternly. 'I will do no such thing. Now that you tell me this whole business is illegal, I don't want to leave any trace of my identity. I will call you later today.'

'Oh madam, you can trust us. We will not reveal your phone number,' said Murtuza bhai, fixing his son with an intimidating stare as he failed yet again to contact the source.

'I don't want to take any chances.' Mrs Ghosh flashed a fake smile as she turned to leave.

'What about an advance payment?' Murtuza bhai followed her.

'I won't pay an advance,' Paromita Ghosh held up her palm. 'I must first see the turtles. I'm not paying you a naya paisa before that!'

'No problem, madam,' Murtuza bhai gave in without protest, 'You can be assured that we will be working on your order immediately.' He snapped his fingers at his son, as if ordering him to get moving at once. 'Please call me this evening. I will have the turtles delivered to you tomorrow along with everything you will need for their care and transportation.'

'Thank you,' said Mrs Ghosh curtly, then turned around and walked out of the store.

Emerging onto the street, the three pet customers took a deep breath, then exchanged quiet glances.

'I hope he burns in hell!' Paromita Ghosh gritted her teeth as they got to her car parked at the end of the street.

'I think Murtuza bhai will be sending Junaid soon to meet the turtle source. Let's wait behind that mango tree there and follow him once he leaves,' suggested Malhar.

'Look, I can't do this,' Paromita Ghosh brought her hand to her head. 'This is too distressing and stressful. I thought it would be fun, a bit of play-acting and all, but no,' she fished out a pill box from her purse. 'I don't have the stomach for this. I can feel my blood pressure rising.'

'You were so brilliant in there, Aunty,' Meera handed her art teacher a water bottle. 'Are you alright?'

'No,' Paromita Ghosh fanned her face with the pallu of her saree after plonking herself on the seat of her car. 'I would like to go home.'

The siblings exchanged anxious glances. Junaid would be leaving soon to meet the turtle source. They absolutely had to give chase. Could they manage it alone?

13

Sweeping Enquiries

'Tell me one thing, Tauji,' Mirchi sat cross-legged beside his paternal uncle inside their little home in Anand Nagar. 'Who sweeps Palm Beach Road?' His brief homework about Keshav Rathi, the seafood businessman, had revealed that the man lived in House No. 52 on Palm Beach Road. Destination determined, the road to get there had occurred naturally thereafter.

Mirchi's uncle, consumed by the newspaper in his hands, paid no attention to his nephew. Head of the Sweepers Association of Maulsari, it was his duty to allot work to those enrolled as sweepers on a contract basis with the municipal council. Nearing retirement now, he held a sway amongst the sweepers and trash collectors in town, for whom he was a sort of patriarch. From settling petty disputes within the community, to obtaining better wages and work conditions for the sweepers, Mirchi's Tauji had done it all, achieving a respectable position in their circle.

'Tauji?' Mirchi gave him a nudge, 'Can you tell me who sweeps Palm Beach Road?'

'Of what concern is that to you?' said Tauji, without looking up from the newspaper.

'You see, I have heard a lot about Palm Beach Road. About the rich people living there, their large bungalows, fancy cars. I was thinking how wonderful it would be to see a place like that at least once before I die.'

'Tch tch...' the uncle fixed him with a glare. 'Such a nautanki you are! Just like your grandmother.'

Mirchi smiled and went on. 'Ordinarily, I'd feel awkward going into a locality like that. But I thought perhaps I can join whoever it is that sweeps the street so I can get a peek into the lives of the rich and wealthy of Maulsari. Please Tauji, allow me to go there on duty once.'

Mirchi's uncle folded the newspaper and put it away. 'Since when did you begin to have such keedas?'

'You see, my new friends at Customs Colony—the SSP Sahib's children,' explained Mirchi, reminding his uncle of his influential friends, 'tell me that their homes are like little huts in comparison to the huge bungalows on Palm Beach Road. Ever since I heard that, I've had this itch to go and see the houses there.'

'You are one hell of a fellow,' smiled the old man. 'You know, when I first saw those houses on Palm Beach Road, I couldn't believe my eyes. And those big fancy cars. I remember once many years ago, I saw the famous actor Suryakanth coming out of one of the houses there. My eyes nearly popped out. I was such a huge fan.'

'So, tell me,' Mirchi grinned, glad to have his uncle's attention. 'Who sweeps the street? Can I go with them?'

'Ah...ugh...' his uncle hesitated. 'It is a strange coincidence that you should ask,' he said. 'Manju is in charge of sweeping Palm Beach Road but has been sick for the last two days. I have already received complaints about garbage piling up on the street. And now with winter and all the falling leaves, the leaf litter needs to be cleared too.'

'I can do that!' Mirchi jumped at the opportunity.

'Soch lo,' his uncle said. 'It's extra work. And I can't pay you the rate Manju is paid. You're not enrolled in the municipal records.'

'Hmm...' Mirchi scrunched up his eyes. 'How much will you pay me?'

'Since you'll be making up for Manju, you will be given half a day's pay.'

'All right,' Mirchi nodded. 'At least I'll get to see this paradise.'

'And don't get into trouble. These people are from a different class of society. None of your silly tricks there.'

'Why would I get into any trouble?' Mirchi stood up to leave.

'And listen, one of the houses there is being broken down for reconstruction. You will have to clear the rubble that has been piling up for two days.'

Mirchi smiled. Construction sites yielded a lot of collectible trash. This was going to be a profitable venture.

'The construction is going on at Bungalow No. 51,' his uncle said, pulling out a little chit from his pocket. 'Make sure you clear up all the debris fatafat!'

Beaming from ear to ear, Mirchi left whistling a song. Lady luck didn't visit him often, but on some days, she just stuck right by his side!

14

A Change of Guard

'Thank you so much for coming so quickly,' Meera ran ahead to the approaching motorbike.

'What's going on?' Isaac pulled up his two-wheeler beside the mango tree outside Domed Market, and took off his helmet.

'Before they fill you in,' Mrs Ghosh took a befuddled Isaac's hand in hers. 'Young man...you have my sincere gratitude. You see, I can't go with them...and I can't let them to go alone. You seem like a responsible fellow. And if I may add, handsome too!' she winked. 'Thank you for being my saviour today.'

'You're most welcome,' Isaac smiled awkwardly as they shook hands. 'I'm sorry...you are?'

'Their art-teacher-turned-partner-in-crime,' smiled Mrs Ghosh, taking her place behind the steering wheel of her car. 'They just called you from my phone,' she said. 'It's a good thing Meera had your phone number noted down in her dairy. Now, you better be careful, kids. Listen to Isaac and do as he says. Nothing silly, alright?'

'What er...are we about to do?' Isaac tugged uneasily at the collar of his plaid blue shirt, having received no more than a sketchy gist of the matter from Meera on the short phone-call.

'Hide!' Meera ducked under the hood of Mrs Ghosh's car and pulled Malhar down with her, adding to Isaac's bewilderment. 'Junaid,' she whispered, 'I just saw him step out of the shop.'

Mrs Ghosh turned her eyes to her rear-view mirror. 'He's starting his scooter.'

'We need to follow the man in that shiny red shirt on the scooter,' Meera whispered to Isaac who was peering through his sunglasses in the direction of the market.

'He's going to meet a big turtle supplier,' added Malhar, pulling out his rucksack from the car, into which he'd packed odds and ends to put on a quick disguise, should the need arise.

'Alright, hop on!' Isaac kickstarted his bike.

'Very well, then,' Mrs Ghosh closed the door of her car, started the ignition, and held up her thumb. 'All the best.'

15

Business as Usual

Mirchi stared at the street that stretched before him. Palm Beach Road was nothing like anything he had seen. Neat tree-lined lanes, clean broad pavements, huge bungalows with imposing walls and expansive lawns, massive gates at each house manned by guards. It looked straight out of a movie scene.

'You see this, Munna?' Mirchi mumbled. 'This is where the richest people of Maulsari live.' He pushed along his garbage trolley. Putting on the florescent orange cleaning bip that his uncle had handed to him, Mirchi slowly eyed the name plates outside the homes and read them with some difficulty. Dropping out of school for two years had slowed down his reading pace.

Captain (Retd) Ranveer Thapa

Brigadier (Retd) Suryavanshi Sinha

Kumaramangalam Aatreya

'Such heavy-duty names, these people have,' Mirchi tittered. 'Look at our names—Mirchi, Kachra, Bablu,

Munna, Manju...and look at theirs! As big as their homes.' He trudged along.

'Look at this,' he said, reading some more name-plates.

Manigandan Ramaswamy

Brigadier (Retd) Kuldeep Singh

Keshav Chandra Rathi

'Ah! There it is. The house we need to watch,' Mirchi stopped right before the gate.

'Woof!' Munna responded as he looked up at the massive structure surrounded by high stone walls.

'Let's keep watch from behind this neem tree,' Mirchi stepped towards the next house. Just as his uncle had said, the neighbouring plot was dug up, surrounded by excavators and trucks. Debris from the broken-down house was piled up at the far end. Pipes and rods, bricks and beams, basins and tap—there was plenty for him to clear. 'This is perfect, Munna! From this position, we will get a good view of Rathi's house. And Dadi is going to be thrilled with my earnings from all that scrap. Proximity to power...' he repeated the snake charmer's words. 'That is our mantra from today.'

'Hey! Hey you!' a gruff voice called out. 'Who are you? And what are you doing here?' A pot-bellied security guard dressed in a bluish-grey uniform came marching ahead.

'I'm here to clean the street,' Mirchi frowned.' Can you not see this orange bip?'

'I've never seen you here before. And where has the cleaning lady been for the last two days?' demanded the watchman.

'The cleaning lady has a name,' said Mirchi. 'She's Manju.'

'Yeah...whatever! Where has she been since Thursday? Look at the street! It's a mess.'

'She's been sick...she's in hospital.'

'Oh! And they've sent you in her place?'

Mirchi nodded, put off by the watchman's attitude. But he'd been careful enough to notice where the man had emerged from—straight out of the imposing Rathi gate. 'Chacha, why do you shout at me?' he said, eager to befriend the fellow. 'I am also a poor labourer like you. We're all here to fill our stomachs.'

The man's expression softened a little. 'Alright alright...get started now. It's nearly noon and there's lots to do. Don't just stand around.'

'Sahib,' said Mirchi, aware that the respectful address would placate him. 'Are you from Gujarat?'

The watchman nodded.

'I could tell from your accent,' Mirchi smiled. 'Me too!'

'Which part?'

'Western Kutch...'

'That's where my wife is from,' the watchman smiled, warming up to the boy.

Nothing cut across strangers in the country like common hometowns and castes. Mirchi knew he had played his cards well. 'Sahib, I haven't eaten since yesterday,' he held a hand over his tummy. 'Any chance you can give me some tea and biscuit?'

The watchman's eyes softened further. 'Hmm... alright. Finish sweeping the street first and then come to that gate. I'll pass you something to eat. But first, clean up properly!'

As the watchman retreated to his post behind the gate, Mirchi rubbed Munna's sides. 'Dekha?' he winked, 'As Dadi says...koshish karne walon ki haar nahi hoti!'

16

Hot Pursuit

Leaving Maulsari behind, Junaid's scooter sped down a road parallel to the state highway, then turned into a bumpy lane.

'Do you know this area?' asked Meera, having finished updating Isaac, as they followed behind Junaid.

'Yeah,' Isaac replied. 'I think he's heading to the shandy.'

'The what?' screamed Malhar, over the sound of the wind hitting their faces.

'The weekly village market,' said Isaac. 'Sometimes we help the forest officials patrol these areas because people bring banned wildlife to sell as meat along with regular poultry in these markets. I think he's headed to meet his source there.'

'What kind of banned wildlife?' asked Meera, as Junaid turned once again into a narrow street.

'Wild boar, hare, monitor lizards...that sort of thing.'

'People eat lizards?' Malhar screwed up his face. 'Ewwwww...'

'Well, its food for a lot of tribal people,' Isaac slowed down as Junaid veered into a crowded market area. 'Not for us to judge.'

'Wow...this market is super crowded,' Meera looked about at the colourful stalls on wheeled carts and sheets spread out on street, displaying an array of items from clothes and bags, to fruits and vegetables, and trinkets to tools.

'He's sure helping us to keep track,' remarked Isaac, 'wearing a shirt that colour! Look, he's stopping,' he slowed down.

'He's making a phone call,' Malhar kept up with his annoying habit of stating the obvious as they watched Junaid. 'And parking. Now he's going into that gate.'

Isaac pulled his bike a little closer, then parked under a gulmohar tree opposite what looked like a row of warehouses into which Junaid had disappeared. 'What now?'

'He mustn't see us,' Meera ducked behind Isaac.

'So what? We just wait here now?' Isaac shrugged. 'For him to get back to his scooter?'

'What if his source doesn't come back with him? We need to see his source!' Meera reminded him.

'Right,' nodded Isaac, cradling his helmet under his armpit. 'You wait here. I will follow him. He won't recognize me.'

'Wrong,' Malhar jumped ahead, his hands on his hips. 'You wait here. I will follow him. He won't recognize me!'

17

An Advocate's Appointment

'Thank you, madam,' Shimplya folded his hands, standing nervously at advocate Madhavi Pradhan's door. 'We are most grateful.'

'Please come in,' smiled Madhavi Pradhan. 'Sit down.'

Shimplya, his cousin Porya, and their uncle whom they called Kaka, stepped in hesitantly, then sat on the floor.

'Oh no, please sit on the chairs,' Mrs Pradhan stood up.

Getting up from the floor, the three of them stared at the lawyer awkwardly.

'Meera and Malhar had said they would be back by afternoon but clearly they have found something more exciting to do than come to their mother's office. That too on a Sunday afternoon!' Mrs Pradhan gestured for them to draw up chairs. 'But don't worry. Please be seated and tell me what has happened.'

Shimplya swallowed hard, feeling awkward to pull up a chair. His older cousin took the lead and all three of them shuffled in.

'My uncle, Surmai Jadhav, has been arrested by the police,' Shimplya's cousin Porya began softly.

'Yes, my children mentioned that. What has he been arrested for? Were you shown the copy of the FIR?'

The three men responded with blank stares.

'The First Information Report,' explained Mrs Pradhan. 'The complaint filed at the police station based on which Jadhav was arrested. Have you seen it?'

The three shook their heads. 'Madam, we do not know anything. The police are not telling us anything clearly. All they say is that he was smuggling turtle hatchlings from the beach. But...' Kaka paused.

'There has been a lot of tension in our fishermen's colony at Anna Nagar over the use of trawlers by fishermen and the killing of turtles,' continued Porya. 'My uncle—Shimplya's father—has often raised his voice against the trawlers. Now suddenly he has been arrested and we suspect this entire affair has something to do with this arrest.'

'Was he produced in court after his arrest?'

'No madam,' the uncle shook his head, 'He was arrested on Friday and we have not seen or heard from him after that. It's been over two days.'

'What evidence do the police have about him smuggling turtles?' Madhavi Pradhan interlocked her fingers on her desk before her.

'They claim to have found a bag of turtles along with cash of Rs 20,000 in his boat.'

'But...but...' Shimplya shifted forward on his seat. 'They are not sea turtles, madam. I was told the pictures show fresh-water turtles. It means...it means that someone has planted the turtles and the money there.'

Mrs Pradhan nodded thoughtfully, throwing open a notepad to jot down the points.

'And madam, think about it, why would someone leave that much cash and the stolen goods in an open boat? No thief would be foolish enough to do that!' added Porya.

'Hmm...' Mrs Pradhan sat back with a sigh. 'I agree. It just doesn't seem to make any sense. Clearly, there is much more than meets the eye!'

18

Donning a Disguise

'Where on earth did you get all this from?' Isaac chuckled, fixing Malhar with an incredulous look.

'I have my sources,' Malhar patted the backpack at his knee, pulled his wig tightly over his head, and ran his fingers through his fake mane of shoulder-length hair.

'So now?' Isaac shook his head, still bewildered over their strange adventure. 'You're going to follow Junaid in disguise?'

'That was the plan.' Malhar's eyes darted this way and that, then he quickly took off his Real Madrid jersey and slipped on a dull moth-infested t-shirt with splotches and stains. 'A good detective is always prepared,' he said.

'Are you sure you're going to be okay?' Isaac eyed the warehouses anxiously.

'I have done this before,' Malhar nodded, patting a mole firmly onto his chin, 'when we solved our previous case.'

'Trust me,' Meera assured Isaac, 'few things excite him as much as putting on a disguise to fool people and snoop around. And like his guru Fatty, he has a ton of this disguise stuff collected over years...and plenty of practice too! Tch,' she glanced at her watch. 'Shimplya will be showing up at Ma's office anytime now,' she sighed. They had planned to be there to introduce Shimplya to their mother. But it looked like they would miss the meeting.

'I need something more, this is not enough,' Malhar mumbled, as he checked himself out in the mirror of Isaac's bike. 'Idea!' he snapped his fingers, then fished out a foldable straw basket from his bag. 'Didi, can you get me bananas from that fruit seller?' he said, opening out the basket and placing it over his head.

Isaac put the bike on the stand. 'I don't feel comfortable about letting you go in alone,' he said, as Meera ran across to the fruit vendor. 'What if something goes wrong?'

'If that happens, it's better that you are out here to help,' said Malhar, patting his hands upon the dry mud by the roadside to give them a hardy appearance. 'Imagine if you go in and something goes wrong...we won't know what to do. We don't even have a mobile phone!'

'And there's less chance of Junaid getting suspicious of a kid selling fruits than some adult snooping about in a place he doesn't belong in,' added Meera, returning with two dozen bananas.

Leaning on his motorbike, Isaac took a closer look at Malhar. With a yellowing old shirt, loose baggy shorts and flimsy rubber chappals, Malhar could pass off as a fruit seller. The mole and wig gave him a completely new look. The old hand-me-down military green cap also gave his face some cover.

'You remember Mirchi? You met him at the police station the other day,' Meera reminded Isaac, emptying the bananas into Malhar's wicker basket. 'Mirchi is a scrap collector. He gets lots of old things that people throw away. So, Malhar has a continuous supply of this junk,' she smiled, reading Isaac's thoughts.

'I've got to admit,' Isaac crossed his hands across his chest. 'I am hugely impressed.'

Malhar smiled, clutching the little basket of bananas over his head with both hands.

'So, what now?' asked Meera, eyeing the block of old buildings into which Junaid had disappeared. With its crumbling moss-covered walls and broken window panes, the place seemed unoccupied.

'I will go closer and look around,' said Malhar, 'and hope to find Junaid's source.'

'Right,' nodded Isaac. 'I will be right here pretending to be a casual visitor to the market. In case you pick up any useful leads or smell trouble, signal to me. Turn your cap around sideways.'

Malhar nodded, his attention consumed by trying to balance the basket on his head.

'And I'll hide behind this row of gulmohar trees,' said Meera, pulling her camera bag over her shoulder, 'and try and get some pictures of the source if he walks out with Junaid.'

'Sounds good,' Isaac patted the kids before they parted ways. 'Let's break a leg, guys!'

19

The Boundaries of Bail

'Appa has done nothing wrong. He could not have,' Shimplya's voice was shaking. 'Madam, my father is a good man,' he said, as his uncle and cousin placed a comforting hand on his shoulder. 'He is being punished for opposing trawlers.'

'Look...if Jadhav has been arrested for committing a bailable offence, bail is granted as a matter of right,' said Mrs Pradhan. 'But if it's a non-bailable offence, one needs to apply for bail and it may or may not be granted.'

The three men exchanged anxious glances.

'I will first need to check up under which section of the law he has been booked. I will have to examine the police diary or the remand application. We have nothing as of now. I don't know exactly what he has been charged with.'

The three stared back with blank faces.

'Well, you appear lost, so let me explain the stages of a case to you. Once a complaint about a crime has been registered at a police station,' explained Madhavi Pradhan in simple terms, 'the police will make inquiries, and then arrest the person whom they suspect in order to investigate the matter. If they want to detain the accused for more than a day, the police must produce this person in court before a judge called a magistrate, and file what is called a remand application, asking that the accused person be remanded or kept in their custody for more time.'

Shimplya gasped. It had been over forty-eight hours since his father had been arrested!

'When the case comes up before the magistrate,' continued Mrs Pradhan, 'the police's lawyer, known as the prosecutor, will have to give reasons to show why the police wish to keep the person in their custody for beyond twenty-four hours. If the magistrate orders the remand, in other words, the detention of the accused, then he may apply for bail, that is, ask that he be released, pending the investigation.'

'So,' said Shimplya with a worried look, 'will my father get bail?'

'Look, that depends on the magistrate and the nature of the case. There is no guarantee of getting bail if he has been accused of a serious offence, which is non-bailable. So I first need to see the remand application filed by the police.'

'And is my father accused of a serious offence which is not bailable?' Shimplya bit his nails.

'I can't say anything at all until I know under what provision of which law he has been arrested,' shrugged Mrs Pradhan. 'If the magistrate orders further detention, we can apply for bail, of course. But the magistrate will take various factors into consideration such as the offence he's accused of, his character, whether he's a first-time offender, and so on. Only then will he decide whether or not to grant bail. Also, if the magistrate decides to grant bail, he may need a surety or bail-bond. You will have to arrange for that.'

'Uh...err...what is that, madam?' asked Porya.

'That means someone trustworthy provides an assurance, taking responsibility that the accused will show up in court when the matter comes up or pay the amount of bail-bond fixed by the magistrate.'

'Okay, so after that, will my father be given bail?'

'I can't say.'

'But my father has not committed any offence!' insisted Shimplya once again, his eyes welling with tears.

'I hear you, beta,' Mrs Pradhan leaned across the table and placed her hand over Shimplaya's. 'We will try our best. But whether he is released or not is not in my hands. That is for the judge to decide.'

20

Human Mule

'Kela lelo!' Malhar managed to call out in a feeble voice, as he walked gingerly past the open rusted metal gate, and inched towards the row of old warehouses. But his voice dried up in his throat as two figures emerged from a building up ahead and made their way straight towards him down a narrow aisle.

Head slightly bent, Malhar managed to catch a quick glimpse of the approaching men. The man on the left was undoubtedly Junaid, unmissable in his glossy red shirt. He was carrying a gunny bag in one hand. His companion, dressed in less flashy attire, was a short man with a distinct bouncy gait. Advancing with halting steps, Malhar's eyes turned to the sack. *Good heavens! Did it contain turtles?* Then his eyes turned to the fast-nearing feet. *What if Junaid saw through his disguise?* He swallowed hard.

On the other side of the metal gate, Isaac ducked behind his motorbike. Pretending to mend the tyre, he had his eyes fixed on Malhar's every move.

Gripping hold of his basket firmly with his sweaty fingers, Malhar took a step ahead. 'Kela lelo, kela,' he called out again, his voice betraying his nervousness. 'Das ka chaar, das ka chaar,' he cried out, like banana vendors he had heard at the market.

As Junaid and his companion got closer, Malhar could sense something amiss. His left hand went to his head. The wig was in place. Then, he reached for the fake mole on his face. It was where it was meant to be. And then, suddenly, it dawned upon him.

'Damn!' he cursed himself. His watch! He had forgotten to take off his watch! No banana seller went about town wearing a fancy Spiderman watch. Besides, there was no doubt Junaid needed no more than a casual glance at the watch to recognize him. He had taken a very good look at it at Anand Nagar yesterday, and at Domed Market this morning.

Heart pounding wildly, Malhar knew he needed to act fast. Holding the basket in place with his right hand, he drew his left hand behind his back, and tried sliding off the strap against his hip. It wouldn't come off! He needed his other hand to undo the strap but there was no time. Junaid was standing right before him.

'Do kela dena,' said that familiar voice.

Malhar's throat went dry.

'Aye...chirkut...can't you hear? Do kela de!' said Junaid gruffly, then turned to show his friend a funny video on his phone.

Making the most of the distraction, Malhar raised his left hand swiftly, and brought the basket to the ground. Then he bent over it to block Junaid's view. Thankfully, the video on the phone had consumed Junaid's attention long enough to give him cover. Grabbing those seconds, Malhar undid the watch and slipped it into his pocket just before Junaid looked up.

'This Bisleri is taking so long. I'm starving, bhai,' Junaid complained to his friend. 'It's way past my lunchtime! When will he be here?'

Relieved to have his watch out of his wrist and inside his pocket, Malhar supressed an impulsive chuckle. *Seriously? They were waiting for some chap named Bisleri?* Ordinarily, that would have had him rolling in laughter. But he kept his eyes down, afraid to look at the two men. As he kneeled over his basket to pick out ripe bananas, his eyes widened. The gunny bag placed at Junaid's feet was moving! *Oh God! So, there was something alive inside!* Trying his best to keep his hands steady, he handed Junaid two bananas.

'How far is it from here?' Junaid asked, peeling the banana and turning to look towards the distant hills.

'About three hours by road,' replied his companion, also turning towards the hills and pointing out the rough route and direction. 'You must come for shikar with us some time,' he said, patting Junaid on his back. 'We can show you how it is done. Just yesterday we shot a wild pig and a hare,' he grinned.

Pocketing the money for the bananas, Malhar shifted uneasily on his feet, his eyes on the gunny bag. Suddenly, a police van turned into the Market Road beyond the gate. Alert to their presence, Junaid's companion appeared visibly on edge and whispered something in Junaid's ear. Keen to stay on and listen to their conversation, Malhar bent down, pretending to arrange the bananas in his basket.

'Hey, you!' a hand grabbed Malhar by the shoulder.

Certain that Junaid had recognized him, Malhar's back stiffened, his neck tensed.

'Chirkut...come along with us!' Junaid ordered Malhar, his eyes pinned on the police jeep slowly winding its way down the busy market.

'Bisleri will be here any time with the stuff,' the companion whispered to Junaid. 'We might need a safe mule.'

'Chal,' Junaid pulled Malhar roughly by his sleeve.

'Where to?' asked Malhar, putting up a brave face, but trembling from within.

'We have some friends over there,' winked Junaid's companion, pointing towards the warehouses as he nudged a nervous Malhar forward. 'They want some bananas.'

Malhar knew the man was fibbing even as he shuffled forward, dragging his basket along. They had said something about making him a mule. Whatever was that supposed to mean?

Outside the gate, Isaac stiffened, sensing trouble. The two men were taking Malhar away with them towards the row of warehouses. He eyed the police jeep that had stopped near the bus-stand. Should he sound an alert and approach the police? Or should he wait and watch? Isaac looked at Malhar closely. The boy's cap was just as it was, facing the front. Or maybe not! Malhar was reaching for his cap. Isaac stood up, ready to make a dash. Then, he sat back down again. Malhar didn't turn the cap to the side as discussed. He simply took it off and put it firmly back on. What was that supposed to mean? Was it a signal to tell Isaac and Meera not to worry? Unable to understand, Isaac nodded to Meera behind the gulmohar tree, indicating that he would follow Malhar at a safe distance.

Alarmed to see her brother being dragged away by two grown men, Meera stopped clicking pictures. Growing fearful and worried, she began biting her nails, and said a silent prayer. *All they had wanted, was to help a poor fisherman. But was that going to get them into trouble?*

21

The Heat is On!

Junaid and his friend walked briskly down the aisle scattered with dry leaves, leading from the gate to the warehouses, pulling along a reluctant Malhar and his basket of bananas. Throwing open a wooden door in the first of a row of large buildings, they entered a room as large as a football field.

Pushing the door shut with the back of his shoe, Junaid took a few steps inside and slumped to the floor, dropping his gunny sack by his side. Placing his basket to one side, Malhar looked around the large room with high ceilings that seemed unused and abandoned. The window panes were dirty and broken, the floor unswept and unclean. Save a bunch of boxes at one end, there was nothing inside.

'Come on up,' Junaid's companion called from a rusty metal stairway leading to a raised platform along one side of the room. Malhar jumped, startled by the echo. 'From the window upstairs, we can keep an eye on the street.'

'Did you call Bisleri?' Junaid, lifted his sack and followed his friend to the mezzanine floor. Malhar trailed quietly behind. 'How will he know where to find us?'

'I have been trying his phone,' said the friend, flicking aside empty cardboard cartons as he walked to the window. 'But it seems to be out of range.'

'Is he coming or what?' Junaid plonked himself under the window.

'He will be here. Have some patience.'

'My father will make kheema out of me if I waste the whole day and return with nothing but these quails,' quipped Junaid.

Malhar glanced at the sack again. *So, that gunny bag had birds?* He listened to the banter between the two, unable to comprehend head or tail of what they were discussing. All he could understand was that there was someone called Bisleri who was expected to show up with something that Junaid wanted. Perhaps the turtles.

Recalling all that Vanaja Narula had explained, Malhar guessed that the companion was perhaps a middleman—a fixer of the deal and the link between the customer in the city and the source of the wildlife in the jungle. *But who was this Bisleri? Was he the carrier? Is that what they referred to as the stuff? What exactly were they taking him along for?* The questions swum about in his head.

'I've been waiting for two hours!' Junaid complained. 'Am I to rely on this Bisleri or what?'

'Hey,' protested his friend. 'Calm down. It's not Maulsari. Dhapchi is a tiny village in the jungle. The buses don't run on time. Sometimes they don't show up at all.'

'Tch!'

'You townspeople think it's all smooth sailing in the interiors like it is for you here. Come there sometime and you will see how hard things are. We don't have electricity or proper roads or hospitals. It takes us an hour to just get to the bus-stop. And then one has to wait endlessly for the bus. It's easy for you to say tch tch. Come there and you will know how hard life is for us.'

'Boss, I'm not here for a lecture about life in the jungle,' Junaid lay down on the floor, tucking his arms behind his head. 'Get me the stuff or I'm leaving.'

'Leave if you like. Yours is not a big order anyway.' Junaid's friend peeped out of the window again. 'It's the other party I am more concerned about.'

'What other party?'

'An overseas party,' said the companion, sticking a toothpick into his mouth. 'The stuff will be going to Bangkok. It's a large order.'

'Tch! And with the police out there,' Junaid clicked his teeth, 'how exactly are you going to bring across this party's big order?'

'We have our ways. Here,' the companion flicked a banana from Malhar's basket to Junaid. 'Have this and cool down.'

Seated on his haunches a few feet away from the duo, Malhar glanced nervously at Junaid, thankful that he was too distracted to pay close attention to him. A bigger deal was going to take place. A larger catch. An international party. More skeletons were tumbling out of the closet.

'The bus is here,' announced Junaid's friend, pointing to a dusty copper-red state transport bus pulling into the bus-stop on the street outside.

Junaid stood up and peered out. Malhar did, too. Dozens of people were pouring out of the bus. Vendors carrying aluminium containers with fresh cucumber and oranges; flower girls with baskets of jasmines and shoe-flowers; knife sharpeners and tool makers; sellers with little wooden boxes around their necks displaying all kinds of ware.

'Can you spot your Bisleri?' asked Junaid.

'No,' replied the companion, whose name Malhar still didn't know. 'But he has sent the stuff. I can see.'

'How do you know?'

'Because the flower girls are here!'

Malhar's ears pricked up. *Flower girls? Had he said flower girls? What did the flower girls have to do with this?*

'They're headed towards the temple,' said the companion. 'You have the cash with you?'

'Yes...but...that blessed police van is parked at the corner,' sighed Junaid. 'I can't go there with this,' he pointed to the sack.

'If the police are patrolling the market, I don't want to take any chances,' the friend cracked his knuckles.

'So what now?'

'That's why we have this chirkut here, don't we?' shrugged the friend, a tad annoyed.

Aware that they were talking about him, Malhar kept his gaze on the floor, his heart pounding as he made a mental note of every clue he'd picked up during the conversation—*Dhapchi village, Bisleri, flower girls, overseas party, Bangkok*. He couldn't make sense of it all, but at least he had the key words. Perhaps if he passed this information on to Vanaja Narula or even Isaac or Akhila, they would be able piece the puzzle together.

A creaking noise below made them all jump. Crawling quietly to the edge of the stairway, they peered out from behind the cardboard boxes. A lean man dressed in dull denims and blue shirt, stylish sunglasses tucked over his head, was inside the warehouse.

Malhar's eyes grew wide. It was Isaac!

'What does this hero want?' Junaid's companion whispered, annoyed by the sudden intrusion.

'Aye Chotu,' Junaid pulled Malhar by the scruff of his neck. 'Now listen to me carefully and do as I say. Or I'll skin you alive!'

22

Breakthrough

'Run down there and tell that pest to beat it,' Junaid held Malhar's shoulder tightly. 'Tell him this is an abandoned warehouse. There's nothing in here for him.'

Malhar nodded.

'And then run to those flower girls outside the temple,' the other continued with the hushed instructions. 'Ask them: *Has Bisleri sent the stuff for Mamu?* And come back straight here with the information. Twenty bucks will be waiting for you.'

Malhar started at the twenty-rupee note being dangled before him.

'Oye, and what about my stuff?' demanded Junaid. 'You're only concerned about your big Bangkok party!'

'Ruk na mere bhai! That will get done too,' the man tutted, before turning to Malhar again. 'Don't mess things up. If the flower girls ask who sent you, say you work for Babban. And be discreet. Ask them if Bisleri has sent the stuff for Mamu. You follow?'

Babban! Malhar finally had the man's name.

'Samjha?'

Malhar nodded and repeated mechanically, 'Babban sent me to check if Bisleri has sent the stuff for Mamu.'

'Shaabash!' Babban gave Malhar a patronizing pat. 'Now go. And leave your basket here.'

'Quickly,' Junaid pushed Malhar along. 'And don't try and act smart,' he added. 'We'll have you roasted for dinner if you try to run.'

Petrified, Malhar hurried to the top of the stairway and made his way down, glad to get away from Junaid.

'There is nothing here, sahib,' he huffed, clattering down the metal steps in a hurry, keen to ensure his voice was audible to the two men in the floor above.

Before a dismayed Isaac could get in a word, Malhar was by his side, squeezing his arm, signalling him to stay quiet. 'There is nothing here, sahib,' he repeated, leading Isaac out through the wooden door. 'This is an empty warehouse.'

'Oh! Ah, I see,' mumbled Isaac, taken aback by Malhar's composure.

'Mechanic, did you say? So you're looking for the mechanic?' Malhar led Isaac away from the building towards the gate.

Isaac scrunched up his eyes but nodded to play along.

'The mechanic's shop is in that direction, sahib,' said Malhar, pointing towards the east as they walked into the aisle leading to the gate.

Having walked a safe distance away from the warehouse building, Malhar whispered. 'Do you see those flower girls outside the temple?'

Isaac's eyes scanned the street. Then he nodded.

'They're carrying the stuff.'

'What?' Isaac's eyebrows narrowed. Was that the courier the wildlife mafia had been using? No wonder they'd never been caught. 'Ah, thank you for leading me to the mechanic,' he smiled. 'Is everything alright?' he switched back to a hushed voice.

Malhar nodded. 'There is a bigger deal happening. Some international party from Bangkok. I have been told to go to the flower girls and ask if they're carrying the stuff.'

'Phew! I was getting worried,' Isaac exhaled hard. 'But you seem to have gathered a lot of information.'

'So, what should I do now?'

Isaac took a deep breath. 'You go on to the flower girls. Make conversation with them as you have been instructed to do and find out who amongst them is carrying the stuff.'

Malhar nodded, his eyes scanning the group of flower girls selling their wares outside the temple at the end of the street.

'I will go to the police patrol party near the bus-stand there, and tell them what we suspect. I'll ask them to help us. In the meantime, you try and get some information on exactly what they are carrying and signal to me.'

'Okay,' whispered Malhar, the butterflies in his stomach taking off for their dance once again.

'Good job!' Isaac added. 'And good luck!' he called out, before parting ways.

As Malhar walked slowly towards the temple, Isaac took a few steps in the other direction, and then as soon as he was lost in the crowd, he turned toward the police jeep. On the way, he stopped to update a worried Meera. 'Malhar is fine. Take pictures of the flower girls.'

'Flower girls?' a puzzled Meera stared at Isaac.

'Flower girls,' repeated Isaac, nodding. 'This may be a big breakthrough. Really big!'

23

Shell-shocked

'Ugh. Hello madam. Good morning madam,' a befuddled Inspector Shevre stood up at attention, shocked to find the wife of the SSP Sahib at his police station.

'It's well past noon now,' smiled Madhavi Pradhan, glancing at her watch.

'Ah yes, of course madam, you are right madam,' Inspector Shevre mumbled, his head spinning. 'What... uh...what brings you here, madam?'

'I'm here to make some enquiries about a client's case. I hope you will be able to provide me with some information on the matter. This is my junior, Alok, who will be assisting me.'

'It would be an honour and pleasure to help you, madam,' Inspector Shevre's chest widened with pride. 'Please...please be seated.'

'You made an arrest on Friday last week,' began Mrs Pradhan, drawing up a chair. 'A fisherman by the name of Surmai Jadhav,' she said, throwing open her notepad.

Inspector Shevre's jaw dropped. Dumbfounded, he stared at the lawyer seated before him. Not in his wildest dreams could he have imagined Madhavi Pradhan to be representing that wretched fisherman.

'I want to know under what section he has been charged,' said the lawyer. 'I would be grateful if you could show Alok the FIR based on which you arrested him, and the police station diary entry.'

Inspector Shevre's throat went dry, his mind in a quandary. How had a poor fisherman like Jadhav managed to hire the services of a high-profile lawyer? That too, the wife of the Senior Superintendent of Police? It made no sense at all! 'May I offer madam and sir some tea or coffee? Or perhaps something cold? Some snacks maybe?' he fumbled, his trembling hands reaching out for the bell on his table.

'Thank you,' replied Mrs Pradhan. 'But if you could provide us with this information, we will get going without keeping you for too long. I know you must be busy. I don't want to be a disturbance.'

'Oh no, not at all, madam, it is no disturbance at all. I'm always at your service,' Inspector Shevre smiled, trying to drown his nervousness in an unending stream of words. 'Some tea for sir and madam,' he snapped his fingers at a constable.

'So, may I see the records in your station diary?' asked Alok, returning to the subject of their inquiry.

'I...I'm not quite sure...which...uh...which case you are referring to,' mumbled the inspector.

'I can understand. I'm sure you handle dozens of cases and can't remember each one,' remarked Mrs Pradhan. 'If you would permit Alok to take a look at the diary, that would be sufficient. We just need to know what the man has been booked for.'

'Please do give me a moment,' Inspector Shevre pushed back his chair and shuffled hurriedly to the next room.

Mrs Pradhan checked the messages on her phone as they waited, even as a figure inched closer from behind her. 'Good evening, ma'am,' a woman's voice made them turn around. 'I am Sub-Inspector Sakhi Pawar. Your children were here on Friday evening to make enquiries about the same fisherman.'

'Ah!' thought Mrs Pradhan. So that is what had prompted all those questions about Wildlife Protection Law over dinner on Friday night. She smiled and greeted the woman.

'I...I...cannot be heard saying this,' Sub-Inspector Sakhi Pawar whispered, 'but the police diary, you can be sure, will have no record of it.'

Mrs Pradhan and Alok looked at each other.

'Shevre Sir is my senior and I really don't have a say in how this police station functions. But I'm only telling you madam that you are wasting your time here.'

Mrs Pradhan frowned, kneading her fingers. Having practised law for several years now, she was aware that things didn't always work the way they were meant to. Police officers often detained and arrested people without keeping a record. More so, in cases involving the poor like Jadhav.

'Thank you, Sakhi,' said Madhavi Pradhan, as she sat back and contemplated the situation. 'Is there any other information you can give me?'

'This is not as simple as it looks,' she stopped abruptly, as Inspector Shevre burst into the room.

'I think madam, the person you speak about, was called in for questioning and sent back home.'

'And I think not,' Mrs Pradhan shook her head, recalling the chilling details of the torture of a poor plumber boy that Meera and Malhar had witnessed at the same police station earlier that year, for which her husband had pulled up and reprimanded Shevre. But it was not her job to teach the inspector how to run his police station. Nevertheless, she couldn't resist the urge to give him a piece of her mind. 'That is not correct!' she said firmly. 'I have just met his family and the man has not returned home for the last two days.'

'You know madam, these people, they...they go on long fishing trips, out for days...'

'He has *not* gone on a fishing trip and you know it as well as I do!'

'He may have...perhaps he is loitering about. You know these people...they get drunk and make a nuisance of themselves making life difficult for others too. If you like, I can make a missing person's complaint. Perhaps he will be found lying about in some gutter somewhere.'

'I *am not here to make a missing person's complaint*!' snapped Mrs Pradhan. 'This man has been picked up by the police two days ago and has not returned home. As far as I know, he was brought to this police station by you Mr Shevre, and he is in your custody.'

'Please calm down, madam,' Inspector Shevre pleaded, beads of sweat dotting his brow.

'Look here, Mr Shevre,' said Madhuri Pradhan sternly. 'I have been instructed to represent this fisherman in court. I need to know under what section he has been charged. You have arrested a man and now you claim to know nothing about him?' Madhavi Pradhan thumped her palms on Shevre's desk, rocking the cups of tea. 'Answer me this Inspector: Is Jadhav in your custody or not?'

'Yes madam!' Inspector Shevre let out a meek reply, buckling under the intense gaze and pressure.

'And why have you arrested him?'

'Sea turtles!' he buckled again. 'He has been detained for possessing and dealing in endangered wildlife and violating the Wildlife Protection Act.'

Mrs Pradhan jotted something into her note-pad.

'Please please understand...sometimes due to burdening work pressure we are unable to enter the details in the police station diary immediately, and we tend to forget. But...' Inspector Shevre tried desperately to defend his actions.

'I take it you will be producing him in court before the magistrate tomorrow?'

Shevre swallowed hard, then reached for a glass of water.

'Look, it is not my duty to explain the law to you. Nor do I harbour the belief that you are unaware of it. But let me remind you in case you have forgotten in your... what did you say...*burdening work pressure*! An arrested person has got to be produced before a magistrate within twenty-four hours of his arrest. You cannot keep him in police custody for more than a day without the court's orders. This should not be news to you.'

Pulling out a handkerchief, Inspector Shevre dabbed at the sweat trickling down his face.

'You arrested him on Friday. The courts were closed on Saturday and Sunday. Tomorrow is Monday. Do you intend to file a remand application seeking further detention of Jadhav?'

Inspector Shevre nodded timidly, like an errant child before a headmaster.

'So, I take it you will be producing this man before the magistrate's court tomorrow?'

Another perfunctory nod. Of all the unexpected turn of events that life had thrown at him, this was amongst the very last he could have anticipated. *How in heaven's name had a godforsaken fisherman like Surmai Jadhav hired the services of a fire-brand lawyer like Madhavi Pradhan?* He just couldn't wrap his head around this.

'Alright then,' Mrs Pradhan rose from the chair. 'See you in court tomorrow.'

24

Under Flower

'Have you got the stuff for Mamu?' Malhar whispered to the first flower girl he came across, sitting in front of the temple steps. She was as tall as him, and dressed in a half-sleeve checked shirt over a bright pink skirt, a thin dupatta thrown over her shoulder. Busy packing gajras of jasmine for a customer, she didn't respond.

'Have you got the stuff for Mamu?' Malhar whispered again, crouching low over her basket. This time she heard him, made eye contact, and held his gaze.

'Pack me some dhruva grass and jaswanti,' a lady broke in, distracting the girl. Malhar stood by, waiting for a response. Glancing in his direction, the girl adjusted her nose-ring, shook her head, and gestured for him to go further.

Gingerly, Malhar walked on to the next girl under a sprawling banyan. 'Have you got the stuff for Mamu?' he asked in a hushed tone. Attending to customers asking for flowers in various combinations, she didn't take any notice of him.

‘Have you got the stuff for Mamu? Babban has sent me,’ said Malhar, hoping the name might catch her attention. It changed nothing.

He walked up the temple steps towards the next girl and repeated the question. She too was occupied with customers, and paid him no attention.

Malhar exhaled hard. There were over a dozen flower girls there. Was he going to have to repeat it with each one? Looking down, he noticed Meera and Isaac approaching the temple with two uniformed policemen. If the flower girls spotted them, they may deny having the stuff, even if they had it. He had to act fast.

He scrutinized the girls’ faces. They were all petite, perhaps not much older than Meera and dressed in a similar fashion—shirt, skirt, dupatta. Each one had a tiny tattoo below their chin, and on their arms too. And they appeared to have something in common—as if they all belonged to the same family or tribe. He looked at their baskets. Were there turtles hidden beneath the flowers? What a superb hiding spot, he thought. No wonder the police and forest officers had not been able to nab the smugglers.

Following his hunch, Malhar decided to approach the girl who appeared to be the oldest amongst them. Dressed in a yellow skirt and peach shirt, she had a certain confidence about her. A big operation would possibly be handed to the most experienced person in a group, he surmised as he walked up to her side. 'Have you got the stuff for Mamu?' he asked in a low voice. The girl's kohl-lined eyes immediately locked with his. Handing her customer some flowers wrapped in dried teak leaves, she made a slight nod.

'Babban has sent me,' whispered Malhar, his heart rate quickening.

The girl's puzzled eyes scanned Malhar from head to toe.

'Has Bisleri sent the stuff with you?' said Malhar, hoping the combination of right words would prompt her to reveal her cards.

Wrapping a bunch of flowers for a customer and pocketing the money in a sling bag across her shoulder, she turned to Malhar. 'Where is Babban?'

Malhar scrunched up his eyes. The girl spoke with a weird accent but he was able to follow enough to know that perhaps they may finally be on to something. 'You tell me first,' he said boldly. 'Have you got the stuff for Mamu?'

The girl looked around to check if they were being watched. Then, she nodded.

'Babban has sent me here to check. I work for him,' added Malhar with an air of confidence.

'Have never seen you before...' the girl pursed her lips.

'The party is waiting,' said Malhar, choosing his words carefully to sound authentic. 'I need to see the stuff and confirm to Babban. Else he will make kheema out of me.'

'I told you,' she repeated through gritted teeth, 'I have the stuff.'

Malhar frowned. The girl's accent made it really hard for him to follow her words. In the crowd, he spotted Isaac watching from behind a large peepal tree at the entrance to the temple complex, two policemen by his side.

'How much for these flowers?' Meera suddenly appeared by his side, pretending to be a passing customer.

'Which ones do you want?' asked the girl.

'The jasmine smells beautiful!' Meera picked out a bunch from the basket. 'But these champas are lovely too. My mother loves to wear the yellow ones in her hair,' she remarked, inhaling the scent of another lot she picked out. 'Oh...I like these too! I'm so confused. Which ones should I take?' she kept jabbering, picking out more and more flowers from the basket.

'Arre! Arre! Don't spoil the flowers,' the flower girl protested, grabbing the flowers back from Meera.

Sensing an opportunity, Malhar crouched near the basket. Isaac and the policemen were moving closer.

'Please,' screamed the girl. 'Don't make a mess of the flowers!' Her voice betrayed her anxiety.

'Oh...you seem to have some more flowers down below!' shrieked Meera in girlish excitement, as her fingers discovered a partition in the basket. 'Can I see those too? I love flowers you see...I would love to buy them all. Oh! How I wish I had a house with a large garden so I could grow all of these in my backyard.'

'Silly girl! Stop at once! You are damaging my flowers!' yelled the flower seller, trying to shield the bottom layer of her basket with her palms.

'Look what you have done,' Malhar decided to join in the charade, admonishing Meera as he put his hands into the basket, pretending to help sort out the flowers. 'You have mixed up all the poor lady's flowers!'

'Oh, I am so sorry,' said Meera, even as she extracted another bunch. 'I really didn't mean to do that.'

With so many hands digging into her basket, the girl was getting anxious. 'Let it be,' she said to both of them. 'I will put them back. I don't need your help.'

'My mother's in the temple,' said Meera. 'I'll be back in a few minutes to buy your lovely flowers and make up for the mess I've made,' she added, before disappearing into the crowd heading towards the temple.

'We better get the stuff out of here before something like this happens again,' the girl whispered to Malhar. 'I don't want to take any more chances.'

Malhar hadn't followed a word she'd said. He nodded anyway. 'Anyone else carrying the stuff?'

'Ratna, Pyari and Mala have some of it in their baskets,' the girl said.

'And are they all here?'

The girl pointed to a mango tree.

'Ok, I'll inform Babban and come back. You wait here.'

'Tell him I want the money first. I'm not handing him the stuff otherwise.'

Once again, Malhar had no clear idea what she'd said but nodded and walked away. Then, mixing into the crowd, he nodded at Isaac. 'Four of them have it,' he whispered, glancing in the direction of the girl at the top of the steps. Their game was up.

Or so he thought!

25

Storm in a Tea-cup

'Thank you, Surendra bhai,' said Mirchi, dipping biscuit into his glass of tea as he sat on an inverted wooden crate in the watchman's booth. 'My stomach has been growling.'

'What is your name?' asked the rotund guard, handing Mirchi some more biscuits.

'Everyone calls me Mirchi.'

'Mirchi? Badhiya!' smiled watchman Surendra Bhandari, walking towards the gate to open it for an approaching car. It was a large white car, the kind of imported car whose spare parts, Mirchi knew, fetched a fortune in the second-hand market. Munna was barking outside, alert to the approaching car.

'Salaam sa'ab!' saluted Surendra, pushing open the gate as the car glided in. From his seat, by the window of the kiosk, Mirchi noticed the man on the back seat. He was in a grey safari suit, large sunglasses over his head, speaking animatedly into his phone. His expression betrayed a sense of urgency. It was Keshav Rathi.

The car drove in and stopped at a tiled porch in front of a large bungalow. Keshav Rathi got off and disappeared into his home.

'Your sahib looks like a wealthy man!' said Mirchi, as Surendra closed the gate.

'They say he is the wealthiest man of Maulsari.'

'What does he do? I mean...I heard from somebody that he wasn't so rich five years ago.'

'He has many businesses,' said the watchman, eager to sound knowledgeable. 'Some in India, some abroad. People from all across the world come to visit him. From Dubai, from London, from Bangkok.'

'What kind of businesses?' Mirchi probed on, dunking his biscuit into the tea.

'Import-export. Fisheries. Construction. Transport...' listed out Surendra, counting each one on his fingers. 'You name it and our sahib is into that business.'

'You are so lucky to work for him,' said Mirchi. 'Do you think I might find a job with him?'

Mirchi pulled his crate-turned-seat closer to his new friend.

'I have a large family to feed, Surendra bhai. My grandparents, my parents, my siblings...they are all dependent on me. I really need a job,' Mirchi spun a sympathetic tale.

'Look, I understand. But there are so many people like you who come here asking for a job. Sahib has no time to entertain such requests. He is a busy man.'

'I can imagine,' nodded Mirchi, 'but surely there must be someone I can speak to. I am willing to do any work—cleaning, loading, packing. I have some experience working as a courier boy too. Could you please find out?'

'Now look here, I felt sorry for you because you said you are hungry. This cup of tea and biscuits is all I can give you. Don't dream of any more help from me.' Surendra jumped up from his stool to open the gate for another approaching car.

Mirchi could hear Munna barking loudly outside. But unlike the last time, the bark at this car was different. The volume was higher, the tone sharper, the frequency greater—enough for Mirchi to know that Munna had recognized someone in the car. Alerted by Munna's distinct bark, Mirchi popped his head out of the kiosk window again. This car was smaller than Rathi's, and unlike that one, it was not chauffeur-driven. Two men were seated in the car, in the front.

'Salaam Mamu!' the watchman saluted one of the occupants as he let it through the gate.

As the car slowed down at the gate for a moment before accelerating, Mirchi scanned the two faces inside. The man at the wheel was the same beefy looking fellow with the enormous moustache who had stood by Rathi's side on the podium at the beach rally. But it was the other man seated beside him, nervously dabbing his face with a handkerchief that caught Mirchi by surprise.

It was a face he knew only all too well. It was Inspector Sanjay Shevre!

26

An Unforeseen Turn

It was chaos and pandemonium all around. Policemen wielding lathis; flower girls hollering for mercy, onlookers demanding answers.

'Why are you harassing us poor people?' wailed the girl Malhar had been talking to. 'We have done nothing wrong!'

'Leave that to us,' said a constable, pulling his belt over his oversized paunch. 'Empty your basket.'

'Look at this injustice,' the girl cried. 'They let the biggest criminals and fraudsters escape from the country while they come after the poor like us.'

'Don't act smart,' the constable yelled back. 'Just do as I say. Empty the basket!'

'Why are you troubling these poor flower girls?' asked a concerned man in the crowd gathering around the fracas.

'I know them,' intervened an elderly lady. 'They have been selling flowers outside the temple here for ages.'

'Please do not interfere in our work,' the senior policeman among them brushed the inquirers aside. 'Move back! Move back, everybody!' he instructed the swelling crowd behind him, taking three large strides forward to steer them away.

'Ouch!' shrieked Meera, pushed to the ground by the force of the crowd. 'Oh no oh no oh noooo!' she hollered, as her camera crashed against the hard stone floor. She picked it up, her eyes filling with tears to see the lens broken, and its glass shattered into pieces.

Meanwhile, making good use of the tree-climbing skills he'd learnt from Mirchi, Malhar had found himself a perch upon the lower branches of a mango tree, where he could enjoy a clear view of the drama over the heads of onlookers, and stay unseen by Junaid and gang. Waiting for the big reveal, he reached into his pocket to check the time. The watch wasn't there! He checked the other pocket. Not there either! He broke into a sweat. Scared of being identified by Junaid, he remembered hurriedly stuffing it into his pocket. *Where had he dropped it?*

'I'm telling you one last time to remove the flowers and empty your basket,' the policeman was warning the flower girl. 'Else, I will have to confiscate your basket and take you to the police station.'

'Take me to the police station for what?' the girl demanded boldly. 'For selling flowers? Is that a crime?'

'Listen here, I am running out of patience. I have information that you are smuggling something illegal in there.'

The crowd gasped. Something illegal in a flower basket? What could it possibly be?

Malhar could see the girl searching for someone in the crowd, a familiar face, someone who could help. Perhaps she was searching for Babban. Or perhaps she was searching for him! But her eyes did not find whoever it was she was looking for. Worried about where he may have dropped his watch, he concealed himself in the lush branches, hoping to stay hidden from the prying eyes of Babban and Junaid.

'Do as you wish,' the girl sat down helplessly beside her basket. 'But if you damage my flowers, you will have to pay me the price.'

At a nod from their superior, two constables began searching the baskets, emptying out the flowers even as the girl beat her chest in anguish. 'Oh, you heartless brutes! You spoil my beautiful flowers by crushing them in your stony hands.'

'A hard morning's work all gone to naught!' another lamented. 'Whoever will buy them from us now? We are ruined and—' she stopped mid-sentence. The crowd let out a gasp.

'So...just selling flowers huh?' the policeman turned to them with a wry smile, as the emptied basket revealed a hidden layer underneath. 'What's inside this?' he demanded, tugging at the plastic sheet separating the top half of the flower basket from the bottom.

The flower girl said nothing, fidgeting anxiously with her hair.

'Move back, move away,' the constable banged his lathi on the ground once again to disperse the curious crowd that had inched closer.

'What is under this sheet?' repeated the constable threateningly.

At another nod from the officer, the constable tore open the sheet. Nearly in tears, the younger flower girls huddled around each other and held hands. The older girl stood fearlessly facing the policemen.

Gathering the broken pieces of her camera, Meera started at the basket. Crossing his hands before him, Isaac held his breath. Up on the mango tree, Malhar could hear his heartbeat.

'What...what is this?' the constable peered at the little packets underneath the sheet. 'This is some gel-like thing!' he said, picking up a packet and examining it closely.

Malhar almost fell off the tree. *Wait! There were no turtles inside the basket*?

'What do you think it is?' the oldest of the flower girls demanded boldly. 'What did you expect to find?' she said, sneering at the policeman's stunned face.

'We thought...that...' the policeman looked quizzically at Isaac. 'We had information that...'

Malhar stared at the basket. What on earth was that material in the plastic packets? Where were the turtles? Is this the *stuff* Babban was talking about? Or had there been some mix-up?

'What is this?' the junior Inspector repeated, picking out the yellowish material with his finger and smelling it.

'Dried tree bark,' said the girl. 'And it's not illegal to sell this. At least not in the country I live in,' she snickered.

The constable examined another packet, shaking his head in confusion.

'Huh!' scoffed one of the younger girls, feeling suddenly emboldened. 'After selling the flowers outside the temple, we sell this to perfume makers.'

'Oh,' the constable sighed, putting the flowers back into the baskets, even as the girls grumbled, demanding compensation for their losses.

The policemen looked at Isaac, who shrugged in return, his eyes searching for Malhar.

Ensconced between the branches of the tree, Malhar held his head in his hands, feeling plain stupid. How had this happened? Was it their accent? Perhaps they'd said one thing, and he'd understood it to mean something else.

Somewhere in the crowd, Babban heaved a sigh of relief. This had been close. Very very close!

Still hiding inside the warehouse, as the late afternoon shadows advanced, Junaid's eyes caught sight of a red object behind a carton by the window. He crept closer, then picked it up in his hands. His jaw dropped open and his eyes grew large in disbelief. He had absolutely no difficulty remembering exactly where he had seen that Spider-Man watch before!

27

Recalibration

'What on earth was Inspector Shevre doing in Keshav Rathi's house?' Isaac scratched his chin.

The M4 were seated in the tiny office of the Maulsari Wildlife Conservation Trust opposite the busy Central Railway Station. Having heard about their turtle-poacher-tracking adventure from Isaac, his biologist friend Akhila had invited them to her office to know all about it.

'Beats me,' said Akhila, looking intently at Mirchi. 'This information adds a new twist to the tale.'

'I not understanding why he coming there,' shrugged Mirchi.

'Maybe they are friends,' suggested Malhar.

'The most unusual of friends,' remarked Isaac. 'Why would a wealthy businessman like Rathi befriend a buffoon of a police inspector like Shevre?'

'Oh no,' said Mirchi, gulping down a samosa that Akhila had ordered. 'They not friends. It looked like they were meeting for the first time.'

'How so?'

'Remember that tall man with long twirly moustache behind Rathi on stage at beach rally?'

Malhar nodded. 'Rathi's bodyguard...'

'He bringing Shevre in car. After they enter gate, he asking Shevre to wait in garden. Then this Muchhad going inside to bring Rathi. Then he introducing them both. Both peoples shaking hands. Our Shevre babu looking very uncomfortable even though he smiling like joker.'

'Hmm,' Akhila nodded, shutting the windows to keep out the construction noise from the road below. 'What happened next?'

'I asking Watchman Surendra bhai who are these people in garden? He telling me Muchhad is Rathi's right-hand man. Everyone calls him Mamu. '

'Mamu!' Malhar stopped rocking the chair. 'Did you say he is called Mamu?'

'Yes! Why?'

'That is the code Babban gave me yesterday!'

'What code?'

'He asked me to go and ask the flower girls if Bisleri had sent the stuff for Mamu.'

'This is getting stranger and stranger,' Akhila stood up and walked about the room.

'Surely there is some connection between this turtle smuggling and Rathi then. It is more than just our suspicion,' Meera tapped her pencil on her blue diary.

'But Mamu—that is such a general name, you know,' Isaac played the devil's advocate. 'We need something more substantial.'

'Ok, what else?' asked Akhila, sitting back down at her desk and flipping open a notepad.

'Rathi's house is like big hotel,' Mirchi continued. 'He having three fancy cars. Many servants running around. Two big foreign dogs. He looking like don of Hindi films, and our Shevre babu looking like a mouse... not very happy...bit nervous. He wiping his head with handkerchief again and again, even while drinking cold drink on cool December evening.'

'Naturally!' exclaimed Meera. 'My mother had just visited him last afternoon and given him a piece of her mind. There was no record of Shimplya's father's detention. He made the record only after my mother went there to make enquiries. She told us all about that after we returned last evening.'

'This is interesting,' Akhila nodded, tapping her notes. 'Your mother goes to the police station and demands to see the records for Surmai Jadhav's arrest. Shevre gets flustered. He then makes his way to Rathi's home immediately along with Rathi's henchman, looking very tense.'

'Now that is a strange chain of events,' Isaac peered at the timeline of the sequence Akhila was jotting down.

'Mirchi's hunch has got to be right,' said Meera 'There is obviously a link between the arrest of Jadhav, the sack of smuggled turtles, and this Keshav Rathi.'

'This is good,' Isaac rubbed his hands. 'I get a feeling we are onto something here.'

'That's what we thought yesterday, too!' Malhar fell back on his chair. 'I just don't know how I got it so wrong. I mean...the girls...their accent was difficult to understand...but I thought I understood.' He kicked his foot against the desk. 'I thought we were going to find turtles under the flower baskets.'

'Relax,' Akhila patted him. 'I have been working with forest-dwelling tribes for some years now, and I still find it hard to follow them most times. What you did was very brave. And besides, now look at the links we are making with all the information Mirchi and you have brought.'

'Absolutely!' added Isaac. 'I can't tell you how impressed I am with your courage and intelligence. Nothing to feel dejected about.'

'But nothing has come of it,' rued Malhar.

'Look, you have helped us unearth some very big links,' Akhila circled words she'd noted in bold in her diary. 'We now know that this Dhapchi village is the source. We know the names of the fixers— one Babban and some chap they call Bisleri. We know that these flower girls are used as couriers. Don't you see, it's all connected. There is a link that joins this part,' she said, pointing to the details of the turtle smuggling in her dairy, 'with that part. It is through one of these fixers or middlemen that the turtles got to Shimplya's father's boat. There can't be too many middlemen operating in the turtle trade in Maulsari. Maybe they were not carrying anything today. But at least we now know their modus operandi.'

'And we also might have a lead to this mysterious Mamu,' added Meera.

'These are very important leads Malhar,' said Akhila, asking her intern to hand the kids some chocolates she'd bought for them. 'Leads that we just did not have until yesterday. Your work has not been in vain.'

'I'm going to Palm Beach Road again today,' said Mirchi, tearing open a wrapper and biting into a bar of Dairy Milk. 'To take construction samaan from next to Rathi house. I am now friend of Surendra—the watchman. I trying to get more jaankaari.'

'That's good. We must keep at it. We can't crack this in one day,' noted Isaac. 'A vital piece of the puzzle is missing. Once we get it, we can put this whole thing together.'

As they sat back imagining what that missing piece might be, Akhila's phone began to buzz.

'What?' she stood up in alarm as she answered the call. 'You can't be serious!' Her face had drained of colour. She listened without saying a word for nearly a minute, then hung up the call, sinking back into her chair.

'What's the matter?' asked Isaac.

'It was the office of the DCF,' she said, her voice low. 'They tested a sample of the material the flower girls were carrying yesterday. The lab report is out.'

'The girls had said it was dried tree bark that they sell to perfume makers,' said Isaac.

'No,' Akhila shook her head. 'It was no tree bark!'

'What was it then?' asked Meera.

'Drugs?' Isaac leaned in.

Akhila pursed her lips and exhaled hard.

'For God's sake! What are you talking about Akhila?'

'It's a new form of smuggling them.'

'Smuggling what?'

'Turtles!'

'Turtles?

'Malhar was right...'

'Wait! That stuff was TURTLES?'

Akhila nodded, her eyes moist. 'It was turtle calipee!'

28

A Matter in Court

'Your Honour, I represent the accused Surmai Jadhav, a poor fisherman who has been wrongfully detained by the police since Friday afternoon.' Dressed in a starched white saree with a white band around her neck, Mrs Pradhan began her arguments, as Meera, Malhar, Mirchi and Paromita Ghosh shuffled into a bench at the back of the courtroom.

Baba Saheb Ambedkar smiled down at them all from a dusty frame behind the judge's podium. The magistrate, a bespectacled grey-haired man in a black suit, perused the bail application on his desk. A middle-aged lady looking thoroughly disinterested in the proceedings typed away into a desktop on his left. A clerk seated below the judge arranged case papers for the day on a long table before him. Dozens of lawyers in black and white stood about, papers in hand, waiting for their case to be called out. Two creaky ceiling fans whirred away above, as Shimplya and his family prayed fervently in the front row, his old grandmother' sobs echoing in the tense room.

'Oh my God!' Meera covered her mouth with her hands, as her eyes settled upon a diminutive man in the witness box up front. 'Is that Shimplya's father?' she asked Mirchi.

Mirchi said nothing, just grit his teeth and clenched his fists as he caught sight of Jadhav. The man could barely open his left eye, his lip had a bleeding gash. Clearly, he had been socked by the police.

'Here's my vakalatnama authorizing me to appear for the accused,' Madhavi Pradhan handed over a sheet of green paper to the magistrate's clerk. 'I have only just been shown a copy of the remand application by which the police seek further detention of my client in their custody for a period of ten days,' she added, holding up another sheet of green paper.

Malhar grimaced, the heavy legal terms sailing over his head. Meera shifted on her seat, recalling a recent case of a famous film star's son who'd been accused of having drugs in his possession. She remembered hearing all these terms in the news—remand, detention, custody. The words were suddenly transforming from meaningless jargon to ideas that affected people's lives.

'Is this the accused?' the magistrate lowered his reading glasses upon his nose to take a better look at Jadhav who was standing with a bowed head and folded hands in the witness box.

'Yes, Your Honour.'

'He appears to be injured.'

'Indeed he is, Your Honour, injuries caused in police custody.'

'Your Honour,' Inspector Shevre sprang forward from behind his lawyer who stood beside Mrs Pradhan. 'The accused already had these injuries when we arrested him on Friday. These injuries were prior to the arrest.'

The magistrate glared at Inspector Shevre. 'Isn't the PP there?' he asked, referring to the public prosecutor, the lawyer who appeared for the police.

'Sorry sir, I mean Your Honour,' Inspector Shevre bent in deference and backed off, nudging his lawyer to speak.

'Your Honour, the accused, he...he already admitted, Your Honour. He confessed,' mumbled Advocate Pramod Kadam, the police lawyer, tugging at the lapels of his black coat. 'His statement admits he had banned wildlife in his possession. We seek...we seek...another week...no, I'm sorry...ten days,' he adjusted his glasses and read from his papers, 'ten more days of police custody to question him thoroughly, Your Honour. So that we may get to understand who is behind this smuggling operation,' he argued, holding up his application. 'Your Honour may be pleased to allow the remand application filed by us, seeking custody of the accused for a further period of one week...I'm sorry...I mean to say...uh...ten days.'

Looking at the bumbling lawyer from the corner of her eye, Madhavi Pradhan picked up a thick book by her side called *Law of Evidence*. 'Your Honour, need I remind an experienced lawyer like Mr Kadam that admissions and confessions made before the police are inadmissible as evidence in court?' she said with a polite nod at her colleague.

'But Your Honour will kindly look at the Seizure Report filed by the police that clearly mentions that cash of about Rs 20,000 and a bag, Your Honour...a bag full of endangered turtles, Your Honour, was found with the accused,' the public prosecutor cut in. 'This is incriminating material that points to the accused's involvement in a massive turtle poaching racket.'

'The Seizure Report, Your Honour, has not been signed by the accused, nor attested by any witnesses, as required under the law. The document is incomplete and inadmissible as evidence,' argued Mrs Pradhan, pointing out flaws in the report submitted by Inspector Shevre about the turtles they claimed to have found on Jadhav's boat. 'In fact, Your Honour, there is good reason to support the contention that my client is being falsely implicated in the case, that his arrest is not bonafide, and that the entire case against him is malicious.'

'What bhaari English your mother is speaking!' Mirchi turned to Meera with big eyes. 'I not understanding anything!'

'She is telling the judge that the police have filed a false case against Shimplya's father,' explained Meera.

'Tch! Why can't she just say it like that?' tutted Malhar. 'Why do they have to make it sound so complicated!'

'Shhhh,' Mrs Ghosh glared at the three of them. 'This is a courtroom. Not a playground!'

They turned back to find the magistrate examining the document before him. He looked up with a sombre face. 'Advocate Pradhan,' he sighed, exchanging a quick glance with Inspector Shevre. 'The accused has been arrested for possessing banned wildlife. Species that are protected under Schedule 1 of the Wildlife Protection Act are accorded the highest level of protection under the law. If found guilty and convicted, he can be sent to jail for up to seven years.'

'Exactly, Your Honour!' Advocate Kadam beamed from ear to ear. 'The matter needs to be investigated, Your Honour. It is a serious offence.'

'Oh bhogoban...I don't like where this is going...' muttered Mrs Ghosh.

'Why judge saying *jail*...' asked Mirchi worriedly. 'What? What happening?'

'The magistrate seems to be siding with the police,' replied Mrs Ghosh.

'Why your mother not saying anything?' Mirchi tugged Meera's arm.

Meera bit her nails, glancing at Shimplya and his tense family in the front row.

‘Is Ma losing the case?’ Malhar’s lips curled downward.

The magistrate nodded. ‘Hmm…I can see…’ he exhaled hard and nodded, agreeing with the submission made by Advocate Kadam. ‘The accused has been arrested for committing a very serious offence.’

29

A Battle of Nerves

'Your Honour will please take note that the accused does not have any previous criminal or police record,' argued Mrs Pradhan. 'He is a respectable member of the fishermen's community in Anna Nagar and will co-operate in every way with the police for further investigation. There is no justification for continued custody.'

'Your Honour!' the public prosecutor sprang up again, after another nudge from Inspector Shevre. 'The accused was in possession of banned wildlife. Your Honour, I submit that only last week, the government issued an alert for sea turtle conservation due to the onset of the turtle breeding season. Releasing the accused would defeat the swift and alert action taken by our police in arresting this poacher. He will tamper with the evidence. He may run away. He may even repeat the offence and—'

'Your Honour,' interjected Madhavi Pradhan, 'if I may be permitted to point out, from the record made available by the police themselves, the turtles allegedly found in my client's boat, are not sea turtles at all! They are in fact fresh-water turtles.'

'Look here,' the magistrate leaned forward, 'these are points concerning the merits of the case. All these details will be taken into account and examined during the trial. We cannot get into all that here at this preliminary stage. At present, we are only concerned with whether the accused needs to be detained in police custody or whether he can be released.'

Shimplya exchanged nervous glances with his cousin Porya in the front row. Far from understanding the nitty-gritty of the law being argued here, even the language of the proceedings was incomprehensible. For, even years after the English had left India, English was the language of the court. In the circumstances, they did the one thing they could. They prayed.

'Indeed, Your Honour,' Mrs Pradhan nodded in agreement. 'Without going into the merits of the case, may I only point out that the arrest has taken place in extremely suspicious circumstances with improper records. The FIR is sketchy, the remand application is shoddy, the seizure report is inadmissible.'

'Wah wah!' Mirchi began to clap, enthralled by the hard-hitting words and great delivery. 'I not understanding anything but that was zabardast Madhavi madam!' He stuck his thumb and index finger into his mouth to let out a whistle, but Meera pulled back his hand just in time.

'Mirchi! Stop!' she said under her breath. 'You can't do this here!'

As all eyes in the courtroom turned back from the two of them, to the judge in the front, Meera felt the hair on her neck standing on edge. She felt incredibly proud to listen to her mother's arguments, watching her hold her own in a courtroom full of men. And yet, she couldn't tell what would become of it all.

'So as I was saying,' Mrs Pradhan continued, 'the accused does not have a previous police record and is a respected citizen. The prosecution has not provided any cause for continued custody, and all their records from the police dairy to the remand application are faulty. There are a number of precedents when this court has denied police custody under similar circumstances. In light of that, Your Honour, I submit that this remand application be disallowed.'

In the front row, Jadhav's wife and his old mother dabbed their moist eyes. As they all awaited the decision, nothing was heard except their sobs, the whirring ceiling fan, and the clattering computer keys of the stenographer.

'Remand application rejected!' announced the magistrate after a long pause, much to everyone's relief, except Inspector Shevre. 'Accused to furnish a bond of Rs 20,000 in court,' he said, placing conditions for the release. Then he shut the case papers and tossed them back onto the clerk's desk, even as Inspector Shevre attempted to mumble something incoherently to change the magistrate's mind. When he realized that the next case had been called and the magistrate was no longer listening to him, he turned away, cursing under his breath.

Shimplya turned his perplexed eyes to Mirchi and his friends in the back, unclear what the magistrate had said, unsure what the words even meant.

Holding up both thumbs, Meera smiled at him and nodded.

'Baba is free! Baba is free!' Shimplya tugged at his grandmother's arm, as they broke into more tears.

'God bless you, my child!' Shimplya's old grandmother called out to the magistrate. 'May God bless you with a long healthy life!'

'Shhhh shhhh shhhh...' Alok, Madhavi Pradhan's junior appeared by her side. 'Please...please. You can't do this. This is a courtroom.' He led them towards the door.

'Baba!' Shimplya ran towards his father, as Jadhav stepped out of the witness box. The fisherman smiled through cut lips, and mumbled a word or two, before the constables took him away.

Meera and Malhar sailed out of the room behind their mother, Mirchi and Mrs Ghosh trundling out behind them. 'Meera! Malhar! Mirchi! Mrs Ghosh!'

Madhavi Pradhan spun around in the corridor. 'So you all managed to find the time to come. Now Mirchi, you can't make a scene like that in court,' Mrs Pradhan smiled, as the Jadhav family emerged behind them. Shimplya's mother fell at Madhavi Pradhan's feet, much to her embarrassment thanking her profusely for taking up this case without charging a fee.

As they stood by listening to Shimplya's family conveying their gratitude, Meera, Malhar and Mirchi felt a gentle tap on their shoulders. It was Shimplya, his eyes brimming with tears. 'Dost...' he said to them, as Mrs Pradhan explained the rest of the procedure to Porya. 'I always praying for your happiness,' he said, wiping his tears with his sleeves. 'Every day of my life, I keeping you always in my prayers.'

30

Closed!

'What on earth is this turtle calipee?' asked Mrs Ghosh, as they made their way to the parking lot of the court. After sending home a teary eyed Shimplya, and seeing off a jubilant Mirchi for yet another afternoon of snooping on Palm Beach Road, they had decided to go once again to the pet shop at Domed Market to make more inquiries, hoping Junaid could lead them to Babban and gang to make one more attempt.

'Akhila told us it is a yellowish gelatinous substance found on the lower shell of turtles. It is the latest way of smuggling out turtles,' replied Meera, glad her mother had gotten busy with another case and not stopped to ask them where they were going.

'Oh Ma,' Mrs Ghosh cupped her face in her palms. 'What and all people do!'

'The lower shell of the turtle is made into this and then smuggled out,' explained Malhar, sliding into the car seat.

'It's a trick the poachers use to get away, and Akhila herself just learnt about it at a seminar on wildlife conservation she attended some weeks ago. Most people—even in the police and Forest Department—don't seem to know about it. The smugglers are using this so the turtles can be taken out unseen and undetected.'

'But what for?' gasped Mrs Ghosh after instructing her driver to go to Domed Market. 'Who wants to buy this turtle coffee?'

'Not coffee, Aunty!' chuckled Malhar, as the car wound its way out of the courthouse. 'Calipee. Calipee!'

'Accha chalo calipee. Why are people interested in buying this thing?'

'Remember Vanaja Narula? The DCF I told you about?' said Meera. 'She explained to us when we met her earlier today that this turtle calipee is sent somehow to West Bengal and from there it crosses the border and goes into Bangladesh. The price of the calipee soars as soon as it leaves Indian borders from a few hundreds to many thousands. It then makes its way to China and the Far East where it is used in medicine and drugs.'

'They even make soup out of it,' said Malhar.

'This is all so unbelievable,' frowned Mrs Ghosh. 'The other day, after coming home from that blessed pet shop, my mind was spinning. That nauseating smell, the sight of those poor creatures all packed into a cage. Oof...I just don't understand this madness.'

'Isaac said he had been involved in wildlife conservation for almost ten years and they still managed to pull wool over his eyes,' said Meera. 'He was as shocked as you are.'

'So, you mean, the flower girls you found at the village shandy were actually carrying this turtle calipee?'

'Yes,' Meera nodded. 'And Malhar had led the police right up to them. But because the police did not know what it was, they let them go.'

'Malhar beta, I cannot tell you how impressed I am,' Mrs Ghosh ran a hand over Malhar's hair. 'Byomkesh babu would have been proud of you,' she said, referring to her favourite sleuth from Bengali literature.

'Absolutely!' Meera added, for once praising her brother without holding back. 'When we visited Vanaja Narula's office with Akhila and Isaac before coming to court, she told us that Malhar had apparently helped them discover more than they had managed to unearth in the last few years. She couldn't stop praising him.'

'But what's the use of all that now?' rued Malhar. 'We've lost that lead.'

'Oh not at all!' Mrs Ghosh put her arm around Malhar, as the car turned into the lane leading to Domed Market. 'Byomkesh da would have told you how crucial the information you obtained was. It will definitely lead to something. Everything will soon fall into place.'

'Madam, the shop is closed,' said the driver, bringing the car to a halt outside Murtuza bhai's pet shop.

‘Just as I had feared. Now this lead is gone too,’ Malhar whimpered.

Meera and Mrs Ghosh looked blankly at the metallic grey shutter that was down and locked. All the other shops on the street were open and appeared busy. Only this one was closed.

‘The shop is closed,’ Isaac said, pulling up to the car window on his bike. ‘I got here about ten minutes ago. Was told by the guy in the hardware store next door that Murtuza bhai hasn’t opened since morning.’

‘Now I’m absolutely sure I dropped my watch in the warehouse.’ Malhar slapped his forehead. ‘Junaid would have recognized it in an instant. They know we are not genuine customers.’

‘Perhaps the shop is closed on Mondays,’ Mrs Ghosh ventured a guess. ‘Some shops are closed on Mondays, you know.’

‘I checked,’ said Isaac. ‘But the hardware guy says Murtuza bhai’s place is open all days of the week. He says it’s unusual for the shop to be closed at this time of the day.’

‘I messed it up,’ Malhar threw himself back on the seat.

‘That leaves us with only one option,’ Isaac said, leaning on the window of the car.

‘What?’ they all turned to him.

‘It’s time to enter the lion’s den!’

31

High Command

The siblings stepped out of the DCF's jeep and stood by a bakul tree. Meera was biting her nails, Malhar jiggling his toes. The sun was about to dip into the horizon and the short winter's day was coming to a close. Birds flitted about busily from branch to branch, looking for a roosting spot for the night. Meera wished she could fly away, while Malhar gazed glumly at the orange ball in the sky.

'Come along,' Vanaja Narula edged them towards the officers' clubhouse.

'This will not work, Mrs Narula,' pleaded Meera. 'Our father will never allow this,'

'Now I know that you know your father well,' Vanaja Narula smiled, 'But I know him too. The police and the Forest Department often work together on many cases and I have always had his co-operation.'

'But we know him better,' Meera protested, taking reluctant steps towards the club. 'He will never agree.'

Neither the Christmas lights strung across the gate, nor the Christmas carols playing on the stereo in the lobby, did anything to cheer her spirits. She barely noticed the large Santa Claus and rotund Snow Man on either side of the enormous Christmas tree at the entrance.

'And we will get into a lot of trouble as well,' Malhar trudged along. 'After we solved a case during the summer holidays, Baba told us very clearly never to do anything like this again. He knows nothing about what we've been up to, and he'll banish us to boarding school if he finds out.'

'Oh don't you worry about that!' Vanaja Narula gave Malhar a reassuring rub on his back. 'You have been a godsend for the Forest Department. I will make sure your Baba does not punish you.'

'I'm not so sure it's that easy to make sure,' mumbled Malhar, pushing open the large glass door of the card room of the Maulsari Officers Club. Always busy, his father seldom got the opportunity to utilize the club facilities. Malhar dreaded the thought of breaking the news of their escapades to Baba on the one evening he'd decided to take it easy after duty, and visit the club for a game of bridge with his friends.

'Ah,' exclaimed Vanaja Narula, 'There he is!'

'Please Mrs Narula, please think over it again,' pleaded Meera. 'Baba had warned us not to play these detective games. He will be very angry.'

'I have thought about it. And this is the only option we have,' replied the DCF, walking spiritedly towards the table occupied by the Senior Superintendent of Police and three others, deeply immersed in a game of bridge.

'Good evening, Officer Pradhan!' Vanaja Narula greeted the SSP. 'It's good to see you taking a break and visiting the club today.'

'Vanaja!' SSP Pradhan exclaimed, before turning in surprise to his children hiding behind her. 'Meera! Malhar! What are the two of you doing here?'

'It's a long story,' Vanaja Narula replied on their behalf. 'Perhaps you can finish your game and then we can talk.'

'Sure. Give me five minutes,' a thoroughly perplexed SSP scratched his moustache and turned back to the cards in his hand.

'Come,' Vanaja Narula said, guiding the children towards the balcony, 'In the meantime, let me get you something to eat.'

Usually, even the thought of grilled sandwiches or chicken tikka masala at the Maulsari Officers Club would have been enough to make Malhar smile. But faced with the impending dressing down from his father, he simply had no appetite.

'You have no idea,' Vanaja Narula said, shaking her head, 'no idea at all how proud your father will be when he hears about all that you have done.'

'No, YOU have no idea,' Malhar felt like saying, throwing a nervous glance at his father, 'No idea at all about how furious my father will be when he hears about all that I have done!'

As they found themselves a table and placed their order, Officer Pradhan walked swiftly up towards them. Malhar reached for the glass of water. Meera rubbed her sweaty palms on her dress.

'So, what brings you all here?' SSP Pradhan pulled up a chair after giving his children a hug. 'Have you ordered your chicken tikka and sandwich yet?'

Malhar shook his head. Chicken tikka was the last thing on his mind. He just wished he could disappear.

'And Vanaja? Pleasant surprise! I know you're not a regular visitor at the club either.'

'Indeed, that is so. I have come here today specially to meet you. I went over to your office and was told you had left for the club. I wanted some permissions from you.'

'From me?' SSP Pradhan exclaimed. 'What permissions?' he asked, calling out to a waiter.

'Permission not as a police officer...' Vanaja Narula paused and hesitated for a few moments. 'But as a parent.'

'My permission as a parent?'

'Your children have been of great service to the Forest Department and I have come here today to request you for permission to allow me to take your son into the Daula forest for conducting an investigation,' replied Vanaja Narula, getting straight to the point.

The SSP stared at the DCF, then turned to Meera, then Malhar with befuddled eyes. 'If you don't mind,' he said, drawing his chair closer, 'Would you care to explain? You see my children don't seem to find the need to tell their father much.'

Meera sensed the irritation in her father's deep voice.

'As I said, it is a long story and I request you, before I begin, to please look at the entire matter kindly,' Vanaja Narula began with a plea of leniency on behalf of the children.

Just as she was about to begin, Madhavi Pradhan strode over to the table. 'Ah, there you all are! I was surprised when I received your message, Vanaja. And came straight here from court. What's going on?'

'You didn't tell me you're coming!' SSP Pradhan remarked, baffled by the sudden appearance of his entire family.

'Pleasant surprise or rude shock?' Madhavi Pradhan laughed, teasing her husband as she pulled up a chair. 'Anyway, thank you Vanaja for the invitation. It's the last court working day before the Christmas break and I'm glad you made a plan to meet. I just didn't realize I'd be meeting you so soon after the tea party again. And my kids...they seem so taken in by you and your forest tales.'

'Yes, so much has been going on. I'm quite overwhelmed myself.'

'Alright now,' SSP Pradhan drummed his fingers restlessly on the table, 'will someone tell me what is going on here?'

'I will. But as I said, please look upon the matter kindly,' said Vanaja Narula yet again. And then, she began her tale.

32

A Difficult Proposition

'So, turtles are being smuggled out of the Daula National Park,' SSP Pradhan stopped Vanaja Narula after the first instalment of her narration. 'And you may be finally onto something. That's great. The police will do its best to help the Forest Department. You can be assured of my co-operation. What have my children got to do with any of this?'

Having laid out the background, Vanaja Narula gestured for Meera to take over.

Exchanging uneasy glances with her brother, Meera swallowed hard and shifted forward in her chair. 'Baba,' she began with a heartfelt appeal, 'we're sorry, we...we didn't mean to upset you with any of this.'

The SSP's eyes narrowed.

Meera began narrating the events of the last few days, starting with when Mirchi had brought along a weeping Shimplya on a dark Friday evening to their house. She told her father about Shimplya's father's arrest at the Sikka Chowki Police Station and their visit the next day to the pet shop in Anand Nagar, their discussions with Akhila and Isaac and all the rest.

As her story progressed, SSP Pradhan's expressions changed from puzzlement to irritation, then irritation to anger. His square face went pale at first, then flushed various shades of pink, before turning red.

'Did you know the children have been running around Maulsari doing all this?' he turned to his wife. 'Just the other day you say the children are enquiring about turtles, and today—this? Had I not told you both to stay out of any such mystery solving nonsense?'

'I am aware,' replied Madhavi Pradhan. 'They are only trying to help a poor fisherman. I appeared for him in court today. The poor chap seems to be caught in some sort of conspiracy.'

'No, actually,' Meera cleared her throat, 'There's more. We visited the pet shop in Domed Market for some leads on the turtle smugglers. Malhar disguised himself and followed the pet shop owner and it led him to the ...'

'What?' both parents asked in unison.

'You never told me any of this!' said the mother.

'Are you both out of your minds?' demanded their father.

Tears stinging his eyes, Malhar couldn't muster the courage to shift his gaze up from the floor.

'Madhavi,' Vanaja Narula took over. 'You will not believe what your son has helped us discover because of his courage. We now know for the first time where the turtles are being smuggled from, the names of the fixers and most of all we also know the route the turtle smugglers are taking to sneak them out right before the eyes of the police and forest guards.'

'You want me to present my son with a gallantry award for being a fool and putting his life in danger?' thundered SSP Pradhan.

'Baba, there was no danger. It was just the pet shop owner and another man,' Meera gulped down half a glass of water.

Malhar continued to stare at the mosaic tiles, wishing they could swallow him up.

'Sir, I am aware the children crossed a line,' explained Vanaja Narula. 'It could have been dangerous. But in their defence, they had nothing but the right intentions. And also, they were careful to involve two adults—their art teacher Mrs Ghosh, and a fellow named Isaac whom I know quite well—both responsible people who would not have let any harm come to the children. And when I got to know all this, frankly, I was quite clear that whatever we do henceforth, has to be done with your knowledge—and Madhavi's.'

'Malhar!' SSP Pradhan wasn't buying any of it. 'What do you know about smugglers to put your life at risk like this? After the idol case last summer, did I not make it explicitly clear to you that you are not to get involved in such things? This is not a game!'

Malhar said nothing.

'I AM TALKING TO YOU!'

'Baba, I am sorry,' hot tears streamed down his flushed cheeks.

'LOOK AT ME!'

'Malhar,' his mother pulled her chair toward him, torn between concern for their safety and admiration for their courage. 'Beta, do you know these smugglers can be very dangerous?'

'I'm sorry, Baba,' Malhar dropped his head onto his mother's lap, unable to face his father. 'I'm sorry...' he wept.

'Baba, we were not trying to solve a crime...' Meera offered a meek explanation. 'We were only trying to help Shimplya find his father...and...uh...one thing led to another...and...uh...'

'Sir, I know it is not for me to say,' Vanaja Narula interjected, 'but I would appeal on his behalf. What he has done is nothing short of pathbreaking.'

'If he is so eager, he can join the force when he grows up,' fumed the SSP. 'I would be a proud father. But this is not the time and age for this sort of stuff.'

'I agree and I totally understand...but...'

'But what?' snapped Dhananjay Pradhan.

'I would ask you to excuse him this one time and...'

Meera held her breath.

'...and also request you for one further indulgence.'

The SSP's bushy eyebrows narrowed.

'Allow me to take him with us into the jungle to identify the fixer.'

'What? Are you mad? You want me to send my eleven-year-old son willingly into the poacher's den?'

'That is the only way.'

'Only way for what?'

'To nab them. We have never been this close. And don't want to lose this chance.'

'What do you mean?'

'We have information that a large consignment intended for a party in Bangkok is being smuggled out. This is our best chance to crack this gang's operations and we must do it before the stuff gets out of our hands.'

SSP Pradhan gave the DCF an incredulous stare.

'The route the turtle trail takes to markets in the Far East is through the porous border with Bangladesh,' continued the DCF. 'To get there, the material must go to West Bengal. The route can be by road, sea, rail, or air, it is difficult to say. As we speak, the material may be getting loaded somewhere to take out of Maulsari. We need to get to it before it leaves our jurisdiction.'

'So why do you need Malhar?'

'The fixer is the only lead we've got to get to the bottom of it. As you perhaps know...' she exchanged a quick look with Meera, 'we uh...had photos of these men...but there was an accident...and the camera got damaged...so we don't have them anymore.'

'Yes, I heard,' said Dhananjay Pradhan crossly. 'A lost watch. A damaged camera. This has been a very costly investigation!'

'They are very sorry for all that,' Vanaja Narula pursed her lips. 'But for the moment, it is important that you can excuse them and allow Malhar to come with us into the forest.'

'What for?'

'Because,' sighed Mrs Narula, 'Only Malhar can identify the fixer, and lead us to the kingpin!'

33

Sweeping Rewards

'Stay a while after you finish work today,' Surendra Bhandari told Mirchi as the boy gathered his collection from the construction site and tied them all together. 'There is a party this evening in the house and there will be much food left over. You can pack some and take it to your family.'

Mirchi waved to the potbellied watchman. 'Thank you, Kaka, you are most kind,' he smiled, having learned the refined ways of the world from Meera and Malhar.

'You've been working all day. Come by for a cup of tea,' the watchman extended Mirchi an invitation, warming up to the boy. 'My job can be lonely and boring. It's nice to have company at times. Come, I'll put a kettle on the stove. It's getting chilly,' he rubbed his hands together before returning to his kiosk.

Mirchi nodded, glad to have another chance to observe Rathi's household. After he'd come from court, he had kept close watch as he'd swept the street and collected waste from the construction site next door. Keshav Rathi had left for work in a black SUV in the morning. His mother had gone out in a white Audi before lunch time. Rathi's children and wife had driven out in a maroon Mercedes a little after that. He'd learnt the names of the cars, made a note of every movement in and out of the house, picking up key pieces of information through casual banter with Surendra Bhandari over cups of tea. As he returned for another cup, he noticed yellow fairy lights strung across trees on the lawn and huge aluminium containers of food being unloaded from a tempo at the back.

'Seems like a big party,' Mirchi slurped his tea, gazing at the large bungalow and garden, as the watchman prepared to stand guard at the gate. *How did people get so wealthy*, Mirchi was lost in thought. On most days, he worked like a donkey, and yet it was barely enough to get by. What was the secret of these ameer-log, he wondered.

Slowly, guests began to trickle in. Mirchi stared longingly at their cars, their fine clothes, their sparkling jewels, at the drinks flowing like water, at the feast fit for a king laid out under a shamiana. A delicious aroma wafted through the cold winter air. Mirchi licked his lips, waiting for a chance to try the chicken legs.

Watchman Surendra had gotten busy, checking every vehicle before letting it through the gate, saluting the visitors, directing them to a parking spot at the back of the house where other drivers stood by, ready to be of service when called. Outside, Munna barked at every approaching car.

'Don't you have anybody to help you?' asked Mirchi, 'you are on duty all day and all night.'

'There is another fellow,' replied Surendra, plonking himself on a stool outside the kiosk. 'But he has gone off to his village. Till he returns, I am on duty round-the-clock,'

'Why don't you get me a temporary job as a watchman to help you?' suggested Mirchi, remembering the snakecharmer, Shambunath's mantra to stay close to people in power. 'I can come here in the evening after school.'

'You remind me of my younger days,' smiled the watchman, rising to attend to yet another approaching car. 'I also pounced at every opportunity like you.'

Munna began to bark. The volume was higher, the tone sharper, the frequency greater. Mirchi knew the occupant of the car even before it had neared the gate. He pulled himself up to the level of the kiosk window to confirm his suspicion. As expected, it was Inspector Shevre. Why was Shevre invited to Rathi's party?

'Salaam Sahib,' Bhandari waved him through. Shevre wasn't dressed in his uniform, but in a gaudy orange shirt, sporting sunglasses even though it had been over an hour since the sun had set, looking quite the clown.

'This policeman was here yesterday as well. Seems like a good friend of your Sahib,' said Mirchi nonchalantly.

'My Sahib is a big man. He has contacts everywhere. Do you know he is now going to stand for elections?'

'My grandmother says money and power make a great combination. Your Sahib will then have both. What party is he going to stand for?'

'You ask too many questions,' Surendra brushed Mirchi aside, as he rose to make way for another car. From Munna's bark, Mirchi knew the occupant was a stranger. He propped himself to look through the window. Two people—a man and a woman, both stylishly dressed—came through in a big car. It was nobody he recognized. But Mirchi made a mental note of their faces anyway.

'Your boss has two fancy dogs...so, he likes pets?' Mirchi tried a different angle.

'Do you know? These are not desi like us,' Surendra replied, settling back down on the little stool. 'They are... err...foreign dogs...from cold countries,' He scratched his head trying to recall the name of the breed. 'The air-conditioning in the house is kept on for them all day!'

'Wah bhai wah!' Mirchi snickered. 'Here we humans are struggling to get two square meals a day and there, dogs are chilling in the AC. What a world!'

'Indeed!' chuckled Surendra as he sprung up from his seat yet again, to allow another vehicle through. He saluted the approaching car as the black-tinted windows were rolled down to reveal a face with Far Eastern features. The man was alone and had come in Rathi's white Audi.

'Who is that?' Mirchi leaned out.

'This is Bada Sahib,' said Surendra. 'From Bangkok! But you don't dream of these fancy places, beta. It's not within your reach—or mine.'

Mirchi's ears pricked up. BANKGOK! He had no idea where in the world it was, but it sounded exactly like what Malhar had mentioned earlier that morning in connection with some big order. *Turtle. Mamu. Bangkok.* This was the third match between Malhar's findings and his. Surely there was a common thread to link it all! 'Does this Sahib not have a car? Why is he using Rathi Sahib's car?'

'Hmm, you seem to be very observant!' noted Surendra. 'Of course, he must have his own car. He is a Bada Sahib after all. But every time he comes, Rathi sir sends him his car as a matter of courtesy to the guest.'

'What business does your Sahib have in Bangkok?' Mirchi prodded further.

'Stop pestering me with so many questions!' Surendra tutted. 'Have you seen a party at a rich man's house before? Look at all that food and all those fine people. Don't bother your little brain with irrelevant matters.'

Not wanting to rouse suspicion, Mirchi turned his attention to the party. Rathi appeared to be introducing Shevre to the man from Bangkok. It looked like they were meeting for the first time. Shevre shook hands with the foreigner and the three of them sat huddled on one side of the lawn, immersed in some serious talk. Each time a bearer came to serve them drinks or snacks, they stopped talking, waiting for the waiter to veer out of earshot, before resuming their chat. It seemed odd, like they were discussing something top secret.

After a while Rathi called out to Mamu aka Muchhad, who appeared instantly by his elbow. At a nod from his master, Muchhad pulled out a packet from the pocket of his kurta, then handed it to a beaming Shevre. Holding up his hand, he beckoned a boy with buck-teeth at the edge of the garden and introduced him to both Shevre and the man from Bangkok. Then, they all listened as only Rathi spoke.

As Mirchi watched the group absorbed in a passionate discussion, his mind began to race. Shevre was there. Rathi was there. A big party from Bangkok was there. *What exactly was going on?*

34

Into the Forest

'So your parents named you well,' smiled Madhavi Pradhan as their car cut through giant teak trees. 'Vanaja means forest-born, isn't it?'

'Yes, my father was in the Forest Service too. So I was literally forest-born,' the DCF smiled, turning her eyes to Dhananjay Pradhan sitting stoically at the back.

'How come people are living inside the forest?' asked Malhar, as the car trundled past a hamlet. 'This Dhapchi village, is it also inside the forest?

'Sounds odd, doesn't it?' smiled Vanaja Narula. 'But it's a very common thing in India. We call them vana grams or forest villages. As I told you earlier, several indigenous tribes have been living within forests—and quite harmoniously so—since time immemorial.'

Meera gazed out at the little huts with low thatched roofs whizzing past her window. *Did the flower girls and their turtle-poaching gang live in houses like this?* Suddenly, she felt uneasy about going after them.

'You see, to the British forests were resources to exploit, and they wanted to control these lands so they could access all the timber there, you know, to build their ships and all that. So, they set up a Forest Department to control our forests and once that came into existence, all these tribals living inside were told to get out. Many were forcibly evicted, some resettled in other areas. But the forest is their home, so they continue to live in close proximity.'

'Now,' Dhananjay Pradhan cleared his throat, finally breaking his silence. 'What is your plan of action for tomorrow?'

'I have alerted my rangers and guards,' Vanaja seemed relieved the SSP was finally participating. 'They will be meeting me at the lodge at seven in the morning, Then we leave for Dhapchi together.'

'Is it safe?' enquired Madhavi Pradhan. 'These poachers, are they armed?'

'No. There has never been a case of armed poaching in the Daula National Park. Our forest guards and rangers are constantly patrolling their beats.'

'Ma,' said Meera, 'these flower girls...you should have seen them. They were poor village girls. Not armed smugglers like you imagine!'

'They are simple people living in the jungle,' nodded Malhar. 'Not gangsters with guns.'

SSP Pradhan shot Malhar a stern glare. 'And what do the two of you know about smugglers and gangsters?

Have you heard about Veerappan who was "a simple person" living in the jungle?'

The children shook their heads.

'That was a different story,' Vanaja Narula clicked her tongue. 'You can be sure there is no Veerappan in these jungles. Else, I would never have planned to take Malhar along for identification.'

'Who is this Veerapan?' asked Meera.

'He is amongst the most notorious wildlife smugglers of India,' said her mother. 'He is known to have killed hundreds of elephants for their ivory and then he smuggled out sandalwood too. But don't worry...Vanaja says there is no such threat here.'

Malhar heaved a sigh of relief. After having heard Babban and seen the flower girls, he had imagined poachers to be poor forest dwellers who had no other source of living. He had no idea poachers could be gangsters with guns. A chill went up his spine.

'And for all your smart thinking,' said the SSP, 'how do you think poachers kill tigers and elephants and rhinos without guns? By physical combat?' he turned away. 'And you two think you're Sherlock Holmes!'

Hurt by the sting in her Baba's words Meera's shoulders slumped. Yes, they had underestimated the dangers of a case like this. Yes, they had not quite understood what it entailed. But they had not set off to tackle smuggling and poaching but to help Shimplya find his father. Who on earth could have anticipated how one thing had led to another? And had they not ultimately helped the police and the Forest Department with their search? Why couldn't Baba give them some credit for that?

Sitting glumly on his seat, Malhar threw his head back and closed his eyes. No! He felt like telling his Baba. No, he wasn't Sherlock Holmes. He was only Malhar. Just eleven years old. And as for Baba...he would soon see how awesome his son really was!

35

Mystery Deepens

Mirchi yawned as the dinner party went on and on. Then he sat up, as the man from Bangkok stood up and shook hands with the others, preparing to leave. 'I must get going,' he said, extricating himself from the little kiosk.

'Arre wait, after all the sahibs leave, you can take some leftovers,' said Bhandari.

'It's too late to take home any food. My folks would have eaten already. You save some chicken legs for me,' he said, his eye on the man from Bangkok, 'I'll eat it tomorrow.'

'Darshan, Sahib ke liye gaadi nikalo,' Mamu instructed a man to call for one of the drivers. Rathi's white Audi emerged into the driveway in less than a minute and the smartly suited man from Bangkok approached.

Mirchi quickly disappeared into the dark alley, whistled to Munna, then hopped on to his cycle. 'You see that foreign Sahib sitting in that big car?' Mirchi whispered into Munna's ears, pointing to the car coming through the gate. 'We've got to tail him!' he patted the mongrel.

As the big white car turned out of the gate, Munna was behind it in a flash. The car began picking up speed on the deserted Palm Beach Road. Mirchi cycled furiously behind it, trying his best to keep up. Munna was yards ahead of him.

From a distance, Mirchi could see the white car turning left. He wondered if there was a shortcut he could take, cut through a parallel road perhaps. But this posh part of town was completely unfamiliar to him, and he did not want to get lost. Pushing harder on the pedal, Mirchi gave chase.

As he reached the curb where the car had turned left, he sighed. The vehicle was nowhere to be seen. Mirchi turned left, then pedalled on, looking for some sign of the white car. Staying on the road, he reached a T-junction that brought the lane to an end.

Mirchi looked left. No sign of the car. Mirchi looked right. No sign there either. He exhaled hard, not knowing where to go.

All was quiet in this part of Maulsari at this hour. The few houses that lined the street appeared to be quiet too. There was no sound of a car having entered those gates. What puzzled Mirchi further was that Munna seemed to have disappeared too!

As he waited at the junction, he noticed dim tail lights in the distance on the road to his right. Squinting, it appeared to him like a big white car. Just as he was about to make a right turn to follow the car, a large black car approached from that side and whizzed past him. Running behind the car in a mad frenzy was Munna!

'Hey!' Mirchi called out to Munna. 'I told you to follow that white car!'

Munna barked as if he were trying to convey something to Mirchi, urging him to tail the black car that had gone the other way.

'What? What is it now? We have no time to waste! Come along,' Mirchi yelled.

Munna continued to bark in the same fashion, facing the direction in which the black car had gone.

'Munna,' Mirchi pressed on with wild hand gestures. 'We need to follow the white car. WHITE CAR! Foreigner man!'

Ignoring his master, Munna dashed off behind the black car.

Mirchi sighed. Then trusting the dog's instincts, he turned his cycle around and followed in the same direction, calling his decision into question every few seconds as he cycled at top speed with the wind against his face.

Up ahead, Munna was racing faster than ever to catch up with the black car. Mirchi could see its tail lights from a distance, as it snaked its way up a slope towards a large gate, overlooking the sea. Huffing and puffing, Mirchi cycled up the incline and found Munna barking and waiting outside what appeared to be a big hotel.

Stepping back, Mirchi read the name displayed outside. Ashoka Palms.

'Munna, you have brought me to the fanciest hotel in Maulsari,' Mirchi gasped, holding his stomach. 'The security guards will kick me out of here if they even set eyes on me.'

Munna continued to bark, still anxious that Mirchi hadn't quite grasped the reason for his detour.

Hiding behind a palm tree, Mirchi peered into the imposing gate across the road. The large black car had drawn up outside a glittering marble porch shining with a dozen bright lights. Two well-dressed guards were holding the door open and much to Mirchi's surprise, the man from Bangkok he had seen at Rathi's house emerged from the back door of the vehicle.

'What?' Mirchi gasped. 'How did he get in there?'

Inside, the man nodded at the guards and quickly disappeared up a set of steps into the hotel.

Mirchi's head swirled, unable to comprehend what exactly had transpired.

'This man was in Rathi's white car just five minutes ago as he turned into the deserted beach road,' Mirchi scratched his head in confusion. 'So somewhere along the way, he switched cars and returned to this hotel in the black car?'

Munna wagged his tail, dangling his long pink tongue, pleased that his master had finally made sense of it all.

'But whatever does that mean, Munna?' Mirchi mumbled, pulling out the little diary that Meera had given him to jot down anything of significance.

71 CC 43

Squinting his eyes, he read the number plate at the back of the car. 'What a strange number that is, Munna,' he said, as he made a careful note of it. He looked up at it again to double check, because he had never seen a number plate so short.

71 CC 43

And this time, he noticed something else that was odd. The number plate was blue.

'I have never seen a blue number plate,' Mirchi said to Munna. 'Taxis and rickshaws have yellow number plates. Private cars have white. What sort of car has blue number plates?' He scratched his head again. He looked at the number plates on the other cars parked on the street. Not one of them was blue! 'Look, Munna,' he said, 'look at the other cars. They all have a pattern. That one—KA 12 PA 1503. Or that one there—MH 03 DA 2954. First state code, then numbers, then letters, then numbers again. But this blue one is so random! I'm sure this fellow is a goon of some kind with a fake car number.'

Knowing the matter merited significance, Mirchi noted this down too.

'You, boy,' a voice called out, making Mirchi jump. With his attention on the car, he hadn't seen a uniformed guard walking right up to him. 'What do you think you're doing here? Get out!'

'Does this road belong to you?' Mirchi glared back.

'Get out at once! You can't sit around begging outside the Ashoka Palms,' the guard warned, raising the stick in his hand.

Munna jumped out of the shadows and barked at the guard.

'Get out!' the guard repeated, holding up his stick, even as he stepped back from Munna.

Mirchi scowled. He hated it when these fancy establishments treated him like dirt. Munna continued to bark menacingly. Watching the guard backing off in fear gave Mirchi something to chuckle about, as he hopped onto his cycle. He whistled and Munna jumped onto the basket in front. 'Good work today, mere sher!' Mirchi pulled out two biscuits from his pocket and offered it to the dog as he cycled off. 'To tell you the truth, I doubted you for a few seconds when I saw you run behind that black car,' he confessed, 'but I'm so glad I followed you,' he said, his eyes on the yellow badge with four stars twinkling around Munna's neck. 'Today, you proved to the world that you are an important member of the M4!'

36

An Adventure, or Nothing!

The first light of dawn revealed the most magical paradise in the stately Victorian jungle lodge, nestled amidst tall trees of arjuna and mahua. The range of rolling hills in the distance, clothed in a blanket of mist, held out an alluring invitation, even as a choir of orioles and koels, robins and bulbuls, chirped to the rhythm of a clear stream that skirted around the cottage. Malhar needed no shaking and waking as he did on school days; Meera was up before her alarm had rung; even the SSP's anger had melted away. Such was the enchantment of the forest.

The siblings emerged from the bedroom and ambled towards the porch from where they could hear voices. Vanaja Narula was up already, speaking to a group of people standing below the steps. 'I will see what can be done,' she was telling them. 'Give me some time.'

'Please madam,' a man in a brown sweater and white turban stood before her with folded hands. 'The blessed boar will destroy all our crops if we don't act fast. It has already damaged so many fields. You have to give us permission to get rid of it.'

'Good morning,' the DCF spotted the children, greeting them chirpily before turning back to the petitioners before her. 'I am busy with another operation today. I promise I will look into it,' she nodded at a guard, who shepherded them away.

'You will give them permission to kill an animal?' Malhar rubbed his eyes as he watched the group leave.

'Wild boars and nilgai,' the DCF led them to a table inside where breakfast had been laid out. 'These are big pests in these areas,' she said. 'Damaging crops and running amok in fields. But the wildlife laws do not permit these people to take matters into their own hands, else they'd be arrested. So they need special permission.'

'And you will give them permission to kill an animal?' Meera stopped short of biting into her apple, perplexed by this strange duty of a forest officer.

The DCF sighed. 'We have tough jobs, don't we?' she smiled at the SSP seated at the table. 'You see, the Forest Department is preventing them from killing the boar,' she told the children. 'So we may have to pay them some compensation. I'll have to visit and see. Anyway...' she pulled up a chair and served them pickle to go with the parathas on their plates. 'From the amla tree growing outside. Try it!'

'Aai would have loved to be here, nai?' Madhavi Pradhan said to her husband as she tried the pickle.

'To be here, she has to first agree to miss her true crime serials!' chuckled the SSP, his mood having lifted considerably since the previous day.

'These photos are so lovely,' said Meera, turning her eyes to the framed pictures of tigers and wild gaur, blackbuck and barasinghas on the walls. She spotted a picture of a group of women and inched closer. 'Is that you?' she said, pointing to a young girl.

'The Green Queens,' smiled the DCF. 'That's what they call women in the field. You see, there were only six girls in my Forest Service batch of forty candidates, because this field...like all else,' she nudged Madhavi Pradhan, 'is still a male bastion. So, we took that picture after we graduated.'

'Is it difficult for women to be forest officers?' Meera sat down and tore into her paratha.

'Not at all,' smiled the DCF. 'You can be whatever you want to be, Meera. Don't let anyone tell you otherwise. I have done it all—walking in waist-deep water full of leeches, trekking in high altitudes with low oxygen, chasing poachers, dangerous smugglers, fighting the timber mafia, illegal miners. I have seen a lot in my twelve years of Forest Service. No difference at all between what a man and woman can do.'

'And what is this?' Malhar winced, pointing to another picture of a princely looking royal standing over bodies of three cheetahs.

‘That’s a photo of the maharaja who is believed to have shot the last cheetah of India, with the three Asiatic cheetahs he killed. It was given to me by one of our instructors at the Forestry Institute in Dehradun, to remind me always of how critical our job is. We have the responsibility to save other species from being wiped out like this.’

Two men in dull buff-coloured shirts came into the room and saluted the DCF. ‘Everyone, meet Babu,’ she introduced the taller of the two men as the cook brought out a tray of piping hot tea. ‘He’s been a forest ranger here for two decades and knows the area well. And this is Shekhar,’ she pointed to the stocky man with a broad hat. ‘He is our reptile expert. Come, join us for breakfast,’ she said.

‘No, it’s ok,’ Babu smiled sheepishly. ‘Ma’am, as per the information you sent us yesterday, the boy’s name is Bisleri,’ he got straight to the matter. ‘If that is so, they’re undoubtedly Pardhis,’ he frowned. ‘Only they give their children such silly names!’

‘Babu,’ Vanaja’s eyes darted to the cook who was now clearing the table, ‘Let’s keep aside our prejudice please.’

‘What is a Pardhi?’ asked Malhar.

‘A tribal community that’s been living in these jungles,’ explained the DCF, ‘and many Pardhis have very unusual names like Bisleri and Button...’

‘Button!’ guffawed Malhar.

'They live in the jungle, Malhar,' whispered Madhavi Pradhan, 'like the hoopoe was a discovery for you this morning, mineral water is a novelty for them. Don't laugh!'

'If you had more time today to chat with our Kheer Singh,' Vanaja Narula patted the cook, concerned that he may have taken offence, 'you'd be surprised at his knowledge of the jungle. He knows every plant, can recognize every pugmark, identify every sound of the jungle. None of us trained in forestry can match up.'

'Thank you, sir,' the cook beamed, before hurrying off into the kitchen.

'He just called you sir!' chuckled Meera.

'Yes, they all do,' nodded the DCF. 'Because they are so used to having male bosses.'

'You can't trust these Pardhis,' Babu reiterated. 'They are criminals...all of them. It's in their blood!'

'Babu, please,' said the DCF, as a curious Meera and Malhar looked on.

'You see,' she explained to the children, 'Pardhis are expert hunters. In the days bygone, they used to help Mughal emperors and other royals in shikar. But when kings stopped hunting, their skills became useless. The British brought in a law to declare them as criminal tribes. And although that law has been reversed now, they continue to live with that shame and stigma. Alright now,' she rolled out a sheet on the table after it had been cleared. 'This is a map of the range we are going to,' she said, gesturing for Shekhar to mark out Dhapchi village.

'You may do what you like, but a leopard will not change its spots, madam,' grunted Babu, returning to his pet peeve.

'Phew!' sighed the DCF, 'Please prepare to get going, Babu. I don't want you in uniform. We will be going in plainclothes.' She took back the marked map from Shekhar.

'Jai Hind!' the two men saluted her and walked out, their steps clattering loudly on the wooden floor.

'This sort of prejudice is so entrenched,' the DCF whispered to the Pradhans. 'Try as I might, it's an impossible wall to break down. Here,' she pulled out two books from behind her and handed them to the siblings.

'*Year of the Weeds*,' Meera read the title.

'*Oonga*,' Malhar read the other.

'Your mother told me you love reading and that's wonderful. But there comes a time when we must grow out of Blyton's pixies and Rowling's wizards and read about real people.' She tapped the books she'd handed them. 'Both these books are for young readers like you, and they will tell you the story of how the Dongaria Kondh tribe of Odisha saved their sacred mountain and forests from a large mining corporation. I hope you like the books. Now, let's get ready to leave,' she rubbed her palms in anticipation. 'An eventful day awaits us!'

Meera nodded, excitement throbbing in her veins. *Would they catch the turtle poachers who'd managed to evade the Forest Department for years?*

Malhar slipped the book into his backpack recalling that when they had solved the Case of the Vanishing Gods, he had been denied the opportunity to join the police raid. But this time, luck was on his side. He couldn't wait for what lay ahead.

As they turned to leave, Meera's eyes fell upon a plaque over the door, containing a quote from Hellen Keller.

LIFE IS EITHER A DARING ADVENTURE OR NOTHING

37

A Faulty Connection

'What are you saying?' Malhar hollered into his mother's mobile. 'We cannot hear you!'

'Arre, I saw a foreigner in Rathi's house,' Mirchi yelled once again, standing with Munna inside a public phone booth.

'Foreigner?' Malhar repeated, the signal in the jungle sketchy and poor. 'Mirchi met a foreigner,' he conveyed to Meera standing by his side, as they prepared to leave for the jungle.

'He is from Bangkok...BANGKOK!' Mirchi raised his voice. 'That man coming from Bangkok...Shevre also with them.'

'Mirchi met a man from Bangkok,' Malhar covered the mobile with his palm and whispered excitedly to Meera. 'Babban had told Junaid about someone from Bangkok! Maybe it was the same guy.'

'They all talking long time in Rathi sahib's house,' said Mirchi. 'Pukka they doing some jhol. Guarantee.'

'Huh...what?'

'JHOL! CHORI! LAFDA!' shouted Mirchi.

'Langda?' Malhar grimaced, before turning again to Meera. 'Mirchi met a man from Bangkok who is lame.'

'Tch! Just give me the phone.' Meera grabbed the mobile from her brother's hand.

'He going big hotel. He having very strange car number,' Mirchi continued, pulling out the little diary from the pocket of his shirt. 'I following him yesterday. Munna helping. Munna best!' He rubbed the dog on the side. 'Hai na Munna?'

'Mirchi, we can't hear you well,' said Meera, nodding at Vanaja Narula who was gesturing for them to get into the car. 'We have to go, we'll call soon. Can't talk to you now!'

And before Mirchi could get in another question or word, the phone line went dead.

38

Sweep Stakes

Chomping down a chilly pakoda, Mirchi kept an eye on the Sikka Chowki Police Station across the road. His observations over the last few days had made one thing abundantly clear to him—Inspector Shevre was the man to watch. Besides, Manju had reported back to duty so he could no longer linger around Keshav Rathi's house. Entering the Ashoka Palms hotel to enquire about the man from Bangkok was ruled out, because nobody would let him near the premises. And the lady on Mrs Pradhan's phone kept repeating that they were out of coverage area...cutting him out from Meera and Malhar. In the circumstances, keeping an eye on Shevre, and treating himself to some pakodas while doing so, seemed like the next best thing to do.

'Shevre Sahib is not inside,' said a constable sipping chai at the gate of the Sikka Chowki Police Station, waving away two policemen who'd approached on a motorbike. 'He's on sick leave.'

Mirchi's ears pricked up. *Shevre was sick? Who were the two policemen on the bike? Why were their uniforms so different?* Folding the remaining pakodas into a newspaper, he casually crossed the street, Munna tailing along behind him as the policeman riding pillion on the bike hopped off and looked about rather puzzled. 'Sick leave?' he asked the constable at the gate.

Blowing into his saucer filled with tea, the constable nodded slightly. 'Kya kaam hai?'

The man did not reply, but turned instead to discuss something with his colleague astride the bike. Then he pulled out his mobile phone and dialled a number, while his companion shut off the bike's engine, got off and walked to the nearby tea-stall.

Slipping his pakoda packet into his pocket, Mirchi moved closer to the man speaking on the phone. Bending down, he slowly picked up plastic bottles lying on the footpath and stuffed them into his sack.

'Accha, ghar pe?' the man said, cupping a hand over his mouth, unaware that he was being watched. Then he signalled to his tea-drinking companion. 'Shevre sahib ke ghar jaana hai,' he called him.

Mirchi scratched his head, wondering if he ought to follow the two men. If Shevre was the man to watch and if he was home, there was little point in waiting here, he thought.

'*Pheeee!*' he whistled to Munna, then jogged to his cycle, preparing to follow the two men with Munna in the basket.

It was an early winter morning and few people except sweepers, and milk and newspaper delivery people were up and about. The motorbike cut quickly through the sleepy streets, leaving Mirchi peddling hard to keep up. After about ten minutes, Mirchi found himself completely out of breath, stopping a few feet away from the bike that had parked outside the Police Housing Colony.

'As if one chase last night wasn't bad enough,' he huffed, stopping some distance away, watching the pillion rider get off and make another phone call. Crouching between a wall and a tempo traveller parked on the road, Mirchi noticed the dilapidated state of the policemen's quarters. 'Even our houses in Anand Nagar are better than this, Munna.' Remembering Meera's instructions, Mirchi then pulled out his little diary to note down the number of the bike, for whatever it was worth.

RPF

ML 03 PA 6152

'Strange,' Mirchi said to himself, 'yesterday I see one odd kind of number plate. Today I see another. I wonder what this means, Munna.'

Looking up from his notebook, he saw Inspector Shevre emerge from one side of the greying building, buttoning his shirt over his big belly. He waved to the two men at the gate, then looked left and right cautiously, before walking up to them.

From where Mirchi stood, he knew he would not be able to hear the conversation. But he didn't have any cover further up on the road, and Shevre was likely to recognize him as the SSP Sahib's children's friend. He stayed low and kept watch.

Shevre first shook hands with the two policemen and discussed something briefly. The pillion rider pulled out a little notepad from his pocket and wrote something into it before checking his watch. Shevre then took out an envelope from his pocket and handed it to the man.

'Aye Munna,' Mirchi's eyes nearly popped out. 'That is the same envelope Mamu gave Shevre last night!'

Munna paid him no heed, his attention consumed by a cat purring on the roof behind him.

The policeman on the motorbike pocketed the envelope, then saluted Shevre before speeding away.

'Tch!' Mirchi clicked his tongue, as he watched the bike getting away. With Shevre still standing at the building gate and talking into his phone, he couldn't bolt out of his spot and chase the bike. It would definitely alert Shevre.

'What on earth does all of this mean?' he scratched his head. 'Inspector Shevre is supposed to be on sick leave but seems perfectly fine! He passes on the envelope he received yesterday to two policemen—but who are dressed in very different uniforms. All of it looks so very suspicious Munna, and I can't make head or tail of it.'

As much as he'd have liked to spend all day trying to unravel the mysterious case, Mirchi feared the thrashing he'd receive from his grandmother if he returned home empty-handed. And that's when it occurred to him. He knew just the right man to help him solve the puzzle!

39

Getting Closer

'Madam, after you called yesterday, I made some inquiries about this village,' Shekhar briefed the DCF as their car made its way towards Dhapchi. 'It is on the banks of Ghomri Nadi, a rich source of fresh-water turtles. And settled mostly with Pardhis.'

'Hmm good,' nodded the DCF, tucking away the walkie-talkie in its holder. 'I've asked for back-up. They'll be arriving in some time. I didn't want a crowd of vehicles at the start. it would have alerted them. Can you see Babu's bike following behind?'

Looking into the rearview mirror, Shekhar nodded, then smiled to notice Meera watching a racket-tailed drongo perched on a silk-cotton tree on his left. 'Look there,' he pointed to a tree trunk on the right, 'A Malabar giant squirrel.'

Meera sighed. *How she missed her camera!*

In the middle seat, Malhar sat huddled between his parents as the cold winter air blasted though a gap in the window. They pointed to a spotted deer in the thicket, then a large group of langurs jumping from branch to branch.

'We're almost there,' Shekhar turned into a dirt road, and the car trundled over giant pebbles in a rivulet, before grinding to a halt outside a mud structure. 'Dhapchi?' he rolled down the glass and asked an old man seated on his haunches under a plantain tree outside his house.

The man gaped at Shekhar, then stared at each face inside the car one by one, and finally at Babu who pulled up on his bike behind the car. Saying nothing, he pointed ahead.

'Ask him how much further,' said the DCF. 'I don't want them to see or hear the vehicle before we get there.'

'How far inside?' asked Shekhar.

A little girl with two pigtails peeped out from the low door of the hut, then said something to those inside. In seconds, five other kids emerged to gape at the big car and its occupants.

The old man bunched the tips of his fingers on his right hand together. 'Panch minute.'

'Let's park somewhere here, then,' said the DCF, looking around to find a suitable spot. 'We can cover the rest on foot.'

As the Pradhan family and the DCF exited the vehicle, they were surrounded by six gawking and giggling children all between two and seven years of age, chattering excitedly in a language none of them could follow. As Shekhar drove off to park the car below a sprawling tamarind tree, Meera took her mother's phone and clicked a picture of the children. Then she turned it around to show them. They squealed in delight. 'Tumhara naam?' she asked, hoping they could follow some Hindi.

'Bottle,' said the boy.

'Bypass,' said another.

'Phatphatia,' replied a third.

'Tarbuj,' smiled the fourth.

'Oh these kids are so adorable,' Madhavi Pradhan cooed, 'and their names are simply delightful.'

Vanaja Narula enquired with the old man if he'd spotted any wild boars in the area lately. He shook his head. 'Bisleri,' she asked the tailing children as they walked down the mud road flanked by dense shrubbery. 'You know him?'

'Arre yeh hai Bisleri.' They all broke into joyous laughter, pointing to the youngest amongst them, no older than two.

'Not this chota one,' smiled Shekhar, catching up with them as they walked towards the village. 'The bada one...'

'I know bada Bisleri,' nodded Bottle.

'Aur phool wali?' enquired Babu. 'Ratna, Pyari...'

Bottle nodded again.

'Take us to these people,' Shekhar told the boy, pulling out a packet from his pocket. 'And this chocolate is yours.'

The boy tried grabbing the wrapper, Shekhar pulled his hand away.

'I can show,' the girl stepped forward.

'I...I...' Bypass and Phatphatia began to jump.

'Chalo, you can all take us,' laughed Babu, cajoling the kids until they came upon a paddy field beside a row of tents and huts. 'But shh...' he hushed, 'Let's stay very quiet until our game is over!'

40

Decoding

'Where did you get all this from?' Aslam bhai looked genuinely pleased as he examined the shiny brass door knobs.

'I don't reveal my sources,' winked Mirchi, emptying more of his prized collection from the construction site on Palm Beach Road onto the dusty floor of the scrap dealer's store in Anand Nagar.

Javed abandoned his task of sorting out plastic bags and turned to Mirchi's sack of goodies.

'Wait till the boys find out about this,' grinned Aslam bhai. 'They'll be following you when you go scrap picking tomorrow!'

'Please don't tell them, bhai,' requested Mirchi. 'In return, I promise to get you better stuff tomorrow.'

Shifting his gaze to the public telephone outside the shop, Mirchi fumbled around in his pocket for the diary. 'You weigh it,' he said to Javed as he stepped towards the phone, 'I'll be watching!'

For the third time since their short and abrupt call that morning, Mirchi dialled the two numbers Meera had given him—Vanaja Narula's and her mother's. But he couldn't get through to either.

Banging down the receiver, Mirchi walked into Aslam Malik's kabadi store and pulled up a stool. None of the scrap collectors had the audacity to do something so bold, but Mirchi had gained a special status after befriending the SSP Sahib's children. Aslam Malik did not complain.

'Tell me one thing, Chacha,' said Mirchi, pulling closer to the scrap dealer who was examining an old discarded music system. 'You get a lot of car spare parts as well, so I'm guessing you should know this.'

Aslam bhai adjusted his glasses as he picked up a smaller screwdriver to open up a CD player.

'Yesterday, I saw a car with a blue numberplate,' Mirchi continued.

'Ruk,' Aslam Malik said to Javed, his attention now on the scrap being weighed by his assistant. 'Show me that,' he said, pointing to a mirror that had emerged from Mirchi's second sack.

'Now I know taxis and autorickshaws have yellow number plates,' Mirchi continued. 'Cars have black and white. Is a blue numberplate fake?'

'Blue, huh?' Aslam Malik ran his fingers along the rose-petalled frame of the mirror.

'Yes, blue plate with white letters.'

'Hmm,' Aslam bhai smiled, pleased with the mirror.

'Is it a fake?'

'Na,' Aslam bhai shook his head, instructing Javed to keep the mirror frame aside.

'Blue numberplate with white letters on a car—is that a fake?' repeated Mirchi.

'Bilkul nahi!' Aslam bhai returned to the music stereo on his desk. 'Blue number plates are for special vehicles. You didn't know that?'

'Special? Matlab?'

'Means cars belonging to Imbashy...Consoolat... International Organization...' his words morphed into various sounds with the betel juice from the paan in his mouth.

'What?' Mirchi asked, comprehending nothing. 'What sea?'

'Arre baba...Imbashy, Consoolaat.'

'Kaunsa laat?'

'Consoolaat... It is the place where those who want to travel, get visas to go out of India.'

'Oh haaan!' Mirchi nodded. 'Con..con...su...Consu...' he tried repeating it so he could recall it correctly when he narrated the events to Meera and Malhar.

'Arre bhai...Consoolaat! Hmm never mind. Such a big word will not enter your little brain.'

'Where Mehrab got a visa to go to Dubai?' said Mirchi, referring to the one instance of a construction worker in Anand Nagar who'd immigrated to the Middle East.

'Haan, now your tube-light seems to have come on,' chuckled Aslam bhai. 'So, cars belonging to these Imbashy and Consulaat people have special numberplates,' he explained.

'Ah,' Mirchi nodded, slowly digesting the information. So perhaps the man from Bangkok worked for a Consulaat then. But why had he felt the need to keep his car waiting for him on a lonely road? Why had he not brought his car to Rathi's house? The questions kept nagging Mirchi, as he fidgeted with the diary.

He rose to make his way to the phone again and noticed two more numbers scribbled in the back of diary. Why had he not thought of them before? He should have called Isaac or Mrs Ghosh!

Dialling Isaac's number first, Mirchi shot one more glance at Aslam bhai.

'Aslam bhai, tell me one more thing. What is the meaning of the letters RPF on the numberplate of a bike?'

'Kya Mirchi, you are friends with the SSP's children and you don't know this much?' Aslam bhai laughed. 'RPF stands for Railway Police Force.'

41

At the Epicentre

'Police!' shrieked a girl in the paddy field, as she spotted the approaching party. 'Police! Run! Run! They've come to get us!'

Jumping into the field, Babu made a dash towards her, even as Meera and Malhar stood frozen in shock. Shekhar ran towards a tent on the right from which a slim boy had popped out his head. Vanaja Narula bolted behind another girl who had started running across the field, as the SSP followed Shekhar towards the huts and tents.

'Malhar, where are you going?' Madhavi Pradhan called after her son as he too made an impulsive dash behind the flower girl in the field. He regretted it almost instantly; the rice crop was nearly as tall as him, and he found it impossible to run in the waterlogged field.

'Stop! Come back!' Vanaja Narula called out after the flower girl. 'No harm will come to you if you cooperate with us!'

Meera stood unmoved by her mother's side in the clearing, chewing her fingernails, even as the children who'd led them there, gathered around her, completely befuddled.

'Bhaago!' the girl's voice cut through the field. Pushing away the tall grass, she ran on. Babu gave chase at twice her speed behind her. She turned to her left. Spotting her bright red dupatta in the sea of green, Babu turned in her direction. She tripped over a bund, then tried to get up. But before she could, Babu had apprehended her.

Behind them, by the time Malhar got to the middle of the field, he was seriously sucking air. That's what all his medals in athletics were worth, he sighed. An untrained village girl could beat him into panting submission! Realizing his pursuit was fruitless, he pulled himself out of the knee-high water and got back to the clearing, leaving the chase to the experts.

As he got there, he noticed his father and Shekhar striding towards them with two young boys wriggling in their grasp. 'We managed to nab these two. Is this Babban?' Shekhar asked Malhar.

When they came near the siblings and Madhavi, they noticed that one of the boys was actually a short man, who only looked like a boy. Malhar nodded, avoiding the man's intense gaze.

'And this is bada Bisleri, isn't he?' he asked the children.

They nodded slightly, perplexed and stunned.

'If you cooperate with us,' Babu warned them, 'you will be shown some leniency.'

'Shame on you!' the flower girl who was still in the same yellow skirt she'd worn when Malhar had met her at the temple, emerged out of the paddy field, Babu dragging her out by her arm. 'You dupe innocent children to catch us. You horrid people! You disgusting heartless brutes,' she spat at Babu, even as she struggled to break free from his iron grip. 'Using our children in your devilish designs. Turning our own young ones against us, luring them with your pathetic sweets and chocolates. Do you not have an ounce of shame or mercy in your stony hearts?'

Meera turned to Bottle and Phatphatia. They were standing by with horror-struck eyes, watching the drama unfold, their beautiful smiles long gone. Her eyes filled with tears, as the reality of it all sunk in. *Had they really used those innocent children*? She felt absolutely rotten, but until that moment, she just hadn't seen things that way.

'We have evidence against you all,' Shekhar gave Bisleri a rough shake. 'We know you've been operating a turtle poaching racket from here. Take our offer and cooperate with us or else you'll spend the rest of your lives in jail.'

'What offer?' the flower girl hit her palms on her forehead. 'Have we not seen all your splendid offers till now? Our homes were taken away, our land, our food, our livelihoods. What else do you want from us now?' she hollered. 'This life is all that's left. Take that away too!' she collapsed in a heap.

'Look,' said Shekhar, 'we know that a large consignment of turtle calipee is being shipped out today. If you turn approver and help us track down your boss who funds and controls this smuggling operation, I assure you, your punishment can be commuted and reduced.'

'We are doomed if we do; doomed if we don't!' mumbled Bisleri, his eyes fixed on the ground as a crowd of villagers began gathering around.

'You horrible sarkari log don't allow us to hunt our food,' the flower girl went on. 'You promise us land and jobs but deliver nothing! Do you have any idea how we pulled through your lockdowns during Covid? It is the jungle that fed us. The jungle that sustained us. Who will care for the jungle more than us? And you big officers come around in your big cars, making us into some wicked poachers out to destroy the jungle.'

'Pardhi, Pardhi they call us everywhere we go,' muttered Babban. 'Criminals. Robbers. Thieves. Nobody trusts us. Nobody gives us a job! Where are we to go?' He too gave up his struggle and dropped to his knees.

Malhar's eyes darted to his sister. She was weeping, her face buried in her mother's shoulder. All the laws she'd learned about, the pride she'd felt about being a wildlife warrior—it all seemed so hollow suddenly. Unfair. Empty. Pointless.

'Look, we're not here to get a lecture from you,' Babu twisted the girl's arm. 'We know a large order is going out to Bangkok. Give us the name of who you are supplying to, and you will walk free.'

'Who believes your false promises?' the girl glared at Babu through fierce eyes. 'My father is a charra cutter and he lost his hand after a leopard attack five years ago. Where is the compensation you promised? All lies!' She spat again as the DCF came panting in, the other flower girl in her custody.

'Managed to obtain some leads from this girl,' said Vanaja Narula, pausing to take in a deep breath. 'They supply turtles to someone called Mamu in Maulsari. This consignment of calipee was delivered to this Mamu's warehouse near the docks. We need to investigate further. Take them all in for questioning,' she instructed a uniformed ranger from the back-up team that was just pulling in.

'Near the docks,' said the SSP. 'Then you should alert the Customs Department. Looks like the consignment is to leave Maulsari by ship.'

'It's going to involve a massive combing operation,' sighed Vanaja Narula. 'Given the scale of operations at Maulsari Port.'

'Yes, once we're out and I have signal, I'll speak to Tripathi in the Directorate of Revenue Intelligence at

Customs,' said the SSP. 'This is your best chance to clamp down on this menace and track the smuggler. We can't let this opportunity go.'

'Right,' Vanaja Narula rested her hands on her knees. 'The most important lead I got from her is...' she held her breath, then looked at her watch, 'the consignment leaves Maulsari tonight!'

42

Turning Turtle

'Are you sure?' Isaac said into the phone, his eyes scrunched up. 'It's Vanaja Narula on the line,' he whispered to the others.

Mirchi jumped up. The call he had been waiting for!

'The docks?' Isaac asked, covering his left ear with his palm to cut out the street noise. 'Sure, I can go there but...' he hesitated, looking down at Mirchi's eager face.

As if the noise of passing trains was not bad enough, the poor signal was adding to the challenge. Mirchi shut the windows behind him, eager to find out how the expedition into the forest had gone.

'What are they saying?' Akhila asked, drawing her chair closer to Isaac's. The deafening sound of the construction work across the street was giving her a headache. The two interns seated along the wall whirled around to listen in.

'They've managed to catch the boys and the flower girls!' Isaac briefed the others excitedly. 'A large consignment of turtles and turtle calipee is being shipped out of Maulsari tonight. They were delivered to the same mysterious Mamu at the warehouse near the docks.'

'Bring it on!' clapped an intern.

'So if Vanaja ma'am is asking us to go to the docks, it's going out by ship?' Akhila flipped open her laptop.

'They're on their way back. I can't hear them clearly,' Isaac moved away from the closed window that was doing little to keep out the din of hooting railway engines and piercing electric drills.

Sensing the excitement in the room, Munna began to bark. Mirchi nuzzled him, trying to calm him down. They already had enough trouble making sense of what was going on.

'Let me check the list of ships leaving Maulsari tonight,' suggested Akhila, peering into her laptop screen.

'Alright, hold on,' Isaac said into the phone, joining Akhila before her laptop. Staring at the screen, Mirchi noticed dozens of rows with lots of words, none of which he could comprehend. All he could read was the title of the page: Indian Customs, Maulsari Port.

'Do you see any ships headed to Bangkok?' Isaac asked Akhila, browsing through the long list, motioning for the interns to help in the search.

Maulsari was a busy port, handling a large part of the country's shipping cargo. Hundreds of ships entered and left daily with several thousand containers of huge tonnage. How were they to search for a small consignment of turtles there? That too, in a matter of hours!

Mirchi glanced at the clock on the wall. It was past four. If the consignment was to leave Maulsari tonight, there wasn't much time left.

'Isaac sir, the train,' he mumbled. 'Narula madam told Meera that turtles smuggled from Bengal to Bangladesh border. And I seeing RPF on bike. Turtles pukka going by train, Isaac sir.'

Holding up his hand, Isaac turned his attention back to the call.

'A ship leaves for Bangkok in two hours,' he replied to Vanaja Narula as an intern pointed to a row on Akhila's screen. 'I will alert Customs immediately.'

Mirchi fidgeted around with a paper clip on the desk. He had a gut feeling about the train.

'Yes ma'am,' Isaac continued, 'I will alert the police station near the docks as well. Do we have a name for Mamu? Whose warehouse am I to complain about?'

Mirchi cracked his knuckles.

'Ma'am, one more thing,' Isaac shifted his gaze to Mirchi, as if to give the boy's theory a chance anyway. 'Meera's friend Mirchi is with us. He uh he has some information which seems to suggest that the consignment may be leaving by train.'

Mirchi straightened up, feeling seen and valued. But the conversation was cut short abruptly from the other side.

'Alright ma'am,' Isaac nodded, dropping his theory like a hot potato. 'We will rush to the docks.' And he hung up the call.

Mirchi's shoulders sagged and he slumped back on the chair like a deflated balloon. Clearly, these adults didn't think his inputs merited any significance.

'So? You have a name for the owner of the warehouse?' Akhila looked up from her screen.

'Nope,' Isaac shook his head. 'The people they arrested didn't give a name. It seems they interact with someone called Mamu. They described him as a tall man with a twirly moustache. That's all.'

'Phir toh koi shak hi nahi hai!' Mirchi snapped his fingers. 'It has to be the Mamu who works for Rathi. It's got to be him!'

'They're bringing them in to help identify this Mamu,' Isaac said. 'But they will take another hour to get here. In the meantime, we need to get in touch with Customs and make sure the consignment is found before it leaves Maulsari.' Isaac gathered his notepad and phone as he prepared to leave. 'Vanaja ma'am wants to catch these guys red-handed!'

'But the train,' Mirchi made one last-ditch attempt. 'Why Shevre sahib meeting two railway policemen and taking packet given by Mamu? It is a bribe!' he insisted.

'Bribe to smuggle turtles. I telling you, Isaac sir. It is going by train!'

'Mirchi, the consignment of calipee and turtles is leaving tonight,' Isaac sighed. 'We have no time to waste.'

'Wahi toh I also saying na,' Mirchi jumped up from the chair. 'I checking already with Ghosh Aunty. She telling me there is train to Kolkata tonight. So we go down to station now,' he pointed to the Maulsari Railway Station premises visible from the window. 'No time wasting.'

Isaac paced up and down the room. Peering through the window pane, he noticed the chaotic railway station across the street, surrounded by construction equipment, dozens of workers, and mounds of mud. That the consignment of illegally poached turtles was leaving Maulsari tonight was confirmed. But was it going to leave by ship or train? Did they have time to check both?

On the one hand, was intelligence obtained from seasoned and trained officials, who had nabbed and questioned the very source of the poaching racket. On the other, a wild suspicion of a young scrap-collecting boy, based on a string of assumptions. Which theory carried more weight?

Glancing at her watch, Akhila shut her laptop and slid it into her bag. 'Get me the phone number of Tripathi at the DRI of Customs Department and text me,' she instructed the interns. 'Isaac, we should get going to Customs immediately.'

'DRI?' mumbled the intern.

'Customs Department is like the police of the docks,' Akhila quickly explained as she grabbed her phone and bag. 'They check all the consignments coming in and going out of the country through ships. The DRI is the Directorate of Revenue Intelligence—a part of Customs that prevents smuggling.'

'Alright Mirchi,' Isaac sighed, going with the momentum. 'We have instructions from Vanaja ma'am and must head to the port and I hope we are right with this lead! But,' he stopped, 'thank you for the great work you've done. I will surely communicate it all to Vanaja ma'am.'

Mirchi frowned. He didn't want a measly certificate of participation or token of thanks. He wanted to catch the smugglers. He kicked the desk as Akhila and Isaac turned to leave, feeling excluded and snubbed.

'Call me in a few hours. I'll tell you how it's going. Okay?' Isaac ruffled the boy's hair before giving Munna a cuddle and disappearing out of the door.

For a few minutes, Mirchi sat glum faced, staring at the backs of the two interns working on their computers. 'Come Munna,' he pulled himself up slowly, 'there is no place for you and me in such hi-fi cases!'

Exiting the building, Mirchi and Munna trudged down the noisy street in a daze, walking past a sea of passengers lugging around suitcases, dozens of coolies pushing around handcarts, and rows of honking autorickshaws and taxis. At the entry gate, a steady stream of people tumbled out of buses and tempos with bags and boxes. In the centre, diggers and cement mixers rumbled away, as workers wearing fluorescent orange bips moved around huge piles of earth and long reams of cable. People. Vehicles. Signs. Luggage. Dust. Noise. The railway station was the most chaotic of all places in Maulsari.

But just as they walked past the station's exit gate, Munna began to bark. Mirchi stopped. It was a bark he knew all too well.

The volume was higher. The tone sharper. The frequency greater.

There was no doubt about it! Munna had recognized someone.

Mirchi spun around and looked at Munna, then at the object of his attention.

A group of people were standing in a circle outside the station's exit gate, beside a mound of dug-out mud. In the centre of the group was a bhel-wala, serving chaat to dozens of waiting customers. Moving closer, Mirchi examined each face there. And then, he saw them!

Two men in railway police uniforms. The very same men he'd seen with Shevre earlier that morning. Gulping away panipuris!

As he caught sight of them, Mirchi's mind began to race. So they wouldn't need to check hundreds of bags and passengers boarding the train to Kolkata, after all. If his suspicion was right, all he needed to do was to keep an eye on those two.

'Shabash, Munna,' he patted the dog and quickened his pace towards the phone booth inside the station, his hawk eyes staying on the two policemen. 'They want to catch the smugglers red-handed, isn't it? Chal beta, that is exactly what you and I will do!'

43

Last Mile

'This better lead somewhere,' an agitated RPF Officer Srikanth glared at Sub-Inspector Sakhi Pawar, who had insisted they had a reliable tip-off about smuggled goods being carried in the 10.30 Maulsari-Howrah Mail.

'It will,' Sub-Inspector Sakhi Pawar nodded, throwing an apprehensive glance at Mirchi, from whom she'd obtained the tip-off, and Meera and Malhar standing by his side.

The children had proved their mettle with a burglary investigation last summer and Sakhi Pawar had every reason to trust them. Besides, she had grown quite fond of them, moved by their compassion for a poor fisherman. So, when she'd received a call two hours ago from Mirchi, she'd harboured no doubts about following it through. More so, with Inspector Shevre off-duty today, and unable to impede things.

For the last hour, every truck, tempo and van that had entered the loading yard of the railway station for the Kolkata-bound train had been examined. Over twenty policemen of the Railway Police Force had been deployed in the search operations.

'No sign of the two policemen you saw earlier?' Sakhi Pawar checked with Mirchi once again.

'I swear I saw them when I called you,' Mirchi pinched his throat. 'But I can't see them now.'

'Obviously the nakabandi and search has scared them away,' Sakhi Pawar nodded, feeling more certain about the tip-off.

'I'm beginning to feel this is also going to lead nowhere,' sighed Meera. 'If the two railway policemen had been paid to let the turtles through, they ought to have been here.'

'What if the police presence has scared them away?' said Malhar. 'Maybe they have informed the smugglers and the consignment won't be sent today.'

'Or perhaps,' Sakhi Pawar presented a counter, 'they have a Plan B, if Plan A does not work.'

'What is Plan B?' asked Meera.

'A back-up plan. If the two have called the smugglers to tip them off about the search and police presence, it is likely they will use another way to get their stuff through. Unlikely they will call it off and bear the cost of delay.'

Just as they pondered about what the back-up plan could be, a big car roared to a halt before them.

A hassled Vanaja Narula stepped out from the front, Shekhar, Babu and Isaac from the rear.

'What have we got here?' Vanaja Narula asked Sakhi Pawar. Exhausted after the long operation and frustrated by the lack of results at the dock, she had lost all hope of finding the consignment until they had received a call from the Sub-Inspector about a search operation underway at the railway station.

'Three hours of search operations launched by the Customs authorities revealed nothing,' Isaac informed the children. 'The ship for Bangkok was thoroughly searched, all its containers put through intense x-rays and every sailor, crew member and storage space on the ship scrutinized. Warehouses that Babban and Bisleri identified as belonging to Mamu were also raided. But we found nothing.'

Sakhi Pawar and Meera quickly narrated the incidents Mirchi had witnessed to Vanaja Narula and the others. Having heard parts of it from Isaac already, she nodded along, glancing suspiciously at the boy. His scraggy appearance didn't evince much faith. Could it be, she wondered. Could it be, that an unkempt slum boy and his dog had managed to crack this ahead of her own team? But this was no time for such musings. She nodded at the Sub-Inspector to continue the search effort, then walked to the RPF officer.

'Mr Srikanth,' she said in a clear voice, 'Thank you for your assistance and cooperation despite it being such a last-minute tip-off. We have every reason to believe a consignment of smuggled wildlife is being taken by the train to Kolkata tonight. This is the closest we have been to cracking this case and don't want to let the opportunity go.'

'I understand, ma'am,' nodded Officer Srikanth. 'We are doing the best we can. But you see the Howrah Mail leaves in twenty minutes. So far, we have found nothing. And it is unlikely that any more goods are to be loaded.'

'Hey, the car,' Mirchi pointed to a vehicle approaching from the gate.

'What car?'

'The car I saw yesterday! The one with the blue numberplate. It's going past the security barricades.'

'It's a consulate car,' Officer Srikanth explained. 'We cannot check it.'

'What?' the children spun around in unison.

'Consulate cars have privileges,' explained Isaac. 'They cannot be stopped and checked.'

'What? But...but...' Mirchi struggled to explain.

'They are cars belong to embassies and consulates of other countries,' said Vanaja Narula. 'They have diplomatic privileges and cannot be searched by the police.'

'Then that's the best way to smuggle something, isn't it?' added Malhar.

‘That’s their plan B!’ Meera turned to Sakhi Pawar. ‘Weren’t we just talking about it?’

‘You mean...you suspect...?’ Vanaja Narula paused mid-sentence.

‘The man from Bangkok who met Rathi yesterday was in that car. Look, same numberplate!’ Mirchi added, pulling out his diary.

‘Oh gosh!’ Vanaja Narula gasped, realizing the import of it all.

‘No wonder they have escaped all surveillance till now,’ Shekhar added. ‘The flower girls and the consulate cars—they are operating under excellent cover.’

‘This is going to get me into trouble,’ Vanaja Narula said under her breath, as she advanced towards the car.

‘Madam! You cannot search that car,’ Officer Srikanth reminded her of the rules, running behind her.

‘Look, Mr Srikanth,’ Vanaja Narula held up her hand. ‘This might be our only chance to nab the kingpin of this operation. I am not letting it go!’

‘But MADAM! It is a breach of protocol.’

Vanaja Narula marched on. ‘I am aware I will be breaking the rules,’ she replied. ‘And I am ready to face the consequences.’

44

Matter of Protocol

A tall man with kohl-lined eyes stepped out from the big black car.

'Mamu!' Mirchi gasped.

The boy with buck-teeth that Mirchi had seen in Rathi's house stepped out after Mamu. Mirchi held his breath.

'I recognize them both,' Mirchi whispered. 'They are Keshav Rathi's men.'

'Please open these bags,' Vanaja Narula ordered the two men, as Sakhi Pawar, Srikanth, Babu, Shekhar and a host of men and women in uniform surrounded the car.

'This is a breach of diplomatic protocol!' a man seated at the back of the car protested, his voice shrill, his accent foreign.

Mirchi tried peeping through the slightly lowered tinted glass, but it was dark inside the car and he couldn't quite tell if it was the same foreigner he'd seen yesterday.

'I am not searching the car,' Vanaja Narula shot back. 'I am searching the bags and boxes you have unloaded from the car. It is no longer covered by diplomatic immunity.'

'Clever,' winked Isaac as Munna wagged his tail animatedly, aware that something immensely exciting was going on.

'I repeat, open the boxes and bags,' Vanaja Narula ordered the men sternly.

Mamu seemed nervous. It was clear he'd been taken by surprise. The younger boy was sweating. They looked caged in.

'Madam, personal baggage,' Mamu said in a weak voice.

'There should be no problem then,' said Shekhar. 'Let us take a look and you can go right through.'

'It's getting late for the train,' said the boy with buck-teeth. 'Our train leaves in five minutes, madam.'

'Howrah Mail—that must be your train?' Babu scanned the nervous faces of the two men.

They nodded awkwardly.

Meanwhile, the man inside the car continued his protests. 'This is a consulate car!' he yelled, threatening to make phone calls to higher-ups and powerful people who would make sure that the officers were stripped off their positions and suspended for life.

The officers exchanged uncertain glances.

'Open up!' Vanaja Narula did not budge.

Frozen, the two men stared back at her.

'Shekhar, Babu, open the boxes and bags.'

Pulling out a pen-knife from his pocket, Babu carefully sliced upon the cover of the first box. Inside it, lining the top, was a sheet. Babu ripped it open, revealing blue plastic bags of various sizes inside. He turned to Vanaja Narula, who motioned to him to open them.

'Madam, the train is about to leave,' the younger boy made one last effort. 'These bags contain fruits. Nothing. Nothing else.'

Babu pulled open two plastic bags.

Stepping forward, Vanaja Narula turned on her torch. The sharp beam of light piercing the dark box revealed the most dreadful of sights.

'Turtles!' gasped Sakhi Pawar.

Turtles! Hundreds of them, packed in layers in little plastic bags, like potatoes in a sack!

'Fruits, huh?' Shekhar grabbed the boy by his collar.

Grimacing, Vanaja Narula shut off the torchlight. The poor creatures, already in undue shock and stress, were recoiling into their shells.

Behind her, Shekhar had opened the other bags, which had revealed little plastic boxes containing the same gelatinous substance Isaac and the children had seen in the baskets carried by the flower girls. There was absolutely no doubt about it. The boxes were full of turtle calipee!

'So, where are you sending these fruits?' Vanaja Narula shot a sarcastic glare at the two men. But even before she'd finished, the boy pushed Shekhar back with his palms, and bolted towards the gate.

'Get hold of him!' Narula ordered the policemen, who were all busy peering into the suitcases and boxes.

The boy skirted around parked bikes and cars as the officers gave chase. Taking advantage of the confusion, Mamu sprang forward, trying to look for a gap in the ring of policemen around him to make an escape.

Suddenly, the engine of the black car roared, and the vehicle began to accelerate.

'We can't let them get away!' screamed Vanaja Narula, taking off behind Mamu.

Railway Police Officer Srikanth began shooting out instructions, ordering his constables to stop the car. Sub-Inspector Sakhi Pawar and her constables chased the running men. As did Isaac. Munna too was behind them in a flash.

Meera looked this way and that. Quickly surveying the situation, she realized that the car would have to drive all the way around the horse-shoe shaped parking ground to get to the exit gate that stood next to the entry gate. 'Come with me!' she said to Malhar and Mirchi, as she squeezed between parked cars to get to the main gate, grateful for the chaos and commotion at the railway station for once.

The driver of the black car was honking furiously, trying desperately to make his way past motionless handcarts and waiting cycle-rickshaws. Squeezing through them all towards the exit gate, the children tugged helplessly at the large wrought-iron structure, trying their best to pull it shut. But the gate wouldn't budge! The rusted structure had been open for years and had perhaps never been pulled shut. Even when all three of them exerted their full force, the stubborn metal gate would just not move.

'What do we do now?' Malhar glanced at the approaching car. It was fifty feet away, blocked only by a rickshaw from which an old woman was disembarking slowly with half a dozen bags. The driver behind her was honking frantically.

'Let's divert the incoming traffic from the entry gate!' said Meera, looking at all the construction signages piled up around her.

'What?' Malhar stared at his sister.

But there was no time to explain. Noticing a large red STOP sign, Meera yanked it out and ran towards the entry gate beside the exit gate.

Taking her cue, Mirchi did the same. Picking up a USE DIVERSION SORRY FOR THE INCONVENIENCE road sign, he placed it before the entry gate. Making sense of Meera's shrewd gameplan, Malhar too picked up a MEN AT WORK signage and plonked it down, the three boards completely blocking the entry gate.

With a frantic wave of their hands, they diverted the incoming cars towards the exit gate.

'Even if one car gets in through the exit gate, it will block the entrance,' Meera glanced ever so anxiously at the consulate car behind the rickshaw. The old lady had gotten out of the rickshaw and was giving the driver of the honking black car a piece of her mind.

Suddenly, there was a spike in the decibel level all around them. Rickshaws hooted, cars honked, motorbikes zipped around. There was utter chaos as vehicles trying to enter the station, found a blocked entry gate.

On the other side of the gate, Vanaja Narula and her team had caught up with Mamu even as Sakhi Pawar and the others had apprehended his accomplice. Meanwhile, the old lady's rickshaw had moved to one side, allowing the consulate car to pass through, and it was now hurtling down the path towards the exit gate. Just then, a large tempo-traveller swerved in. An autorickshaw followed. An Omni was behind them.

As the tempo nosed into the gate, the driver slammed the brakes and its tyres screeched to a sudden halt. 'Fool! What do you think you're doing?' he stuck his neck out of the window, glaring at the black car which had nearly collided into him. 'Are you out of your mind?'

'Hey! What the hell do you think you're doing?' shouted the autorickshaw driver behind the tempo-traveller.

'What an ass!' cursed the driver of the Omni as he braked hard to avoid colliding into the autorickshaw.

Amidst all the frantic braking and shouting, the black car was trapped, and unable to escape.

'Phew!' Meera sighed in relief. Mirchi clapped. Malhar punched his fists into the air, as the officers ran towards the consulate car stopped at the gate. Permissions and paperwork would be required to search the car and its occupant, but at least they had been apprehended and stopped. Mamu, his assistant and the man from Bangkok—all caught red-handed! And the turtles rescued, just in the nick of time.

'Super, guys! Well done!' Vanaja Narula patted the children. The turtle smuggling racket of Maulsari had finally been brought to a close!

45

Home at Last

Aaji said a prayer. Paromita Ghosh wiped a tear. Madhavi Pradhan and the SSP stood by alongside Mirchi's family, feeling immensely proud.

Babu and Shekhar approached the river bank, trays in hand. Rolling up their pants, they stepped nearer the river's edge, balancing the containers between them.

'Wait,' Vanaja Narula instructed them and turned to the M4. After the consignment had been caught and the smugglers apprehended at the station, the next few days had gone by in a whirlwind of activity. Seizure Reports of all the material seized from the bags and boxes had been drawn up. Every turtle had been identified and numbered, photographed and documented.

1280 endangered turtles in all! Out of which 110 had died in the plastic cases out of suffocation.

The boxes with the gelatinous substance had been dispatched to the government laboratory for testing. As suspected, the lab tests had revealed it was turtle calipee, hundreds of kilograms of it obtained by killing thousands of turtles. Meanwhile, the SSP had suspended Inspector Shevre from duty and instituted an enquiry against him.

Not wanting to leave any stone unturned in ensuring that the culprits were brought to book in court, Vanaja Narula had ensured that the evidence collected and documented would make for a water-tight case.

Now, after all the formalities, it was finally time for the homecoming.

'Wait,' Vanaja Narula instructed Babu and Shekhar again, as she walked over to the children swinging on a woody liana nearby. 'Come,' she invited them. 'You must have the honour of releasing the first turtle into the water.'

'The children deserve medals of honour,' remarked Mrs Ghosh. 'Last summer, they contributed to saving our vanishing cultural heritage. This time, our natural heritage. Why, even Byomkesh Bakshi and Sherlock Holmes would have been proud of them!'

The SSP nodded. 'I am proud of the children,' he said after a considered pause. 'And the honour of releasing the first turtle must indeed go to them.'

Malhar punched his fist in the air. Meera beamed. Mirchi did a little jig. One more pat on the back for the M4 from the top cop of Maulsari.

'What you children have done is just unbelievable,' Akhila agreed. 'Not only have you helped these poor turtles, but you've also assisted us all in exposing Rathi—the kingpin of this wildlife mafia in Maulsari.'

'And it is so commendable that this little boy Mirchi decided to take matters in his own hands and not give up till the very end,' added Isaac, turning to Mirchi's parents and grandmother. 'That calls for a lot of courage.'

Mirchi's mother dabbed her moist eyes. Seldom had she heard her boy being showered with praise.

'And don't forget,' said Aaji, 'they helped Shimplya's father too! The poor fisherman would have been languishing in the lock-up had it not been for them.'

'It's not just the children, you know,' smiled Isaac. 'Munna played a big role too!' He put his arms around the dog, adjusting his yellow M4 collar and holding him back from the tray as Meera, Malhar and Mirchi moved closer to the water's edge.

'Woof!' Munna acknowledged the appreciation.

Digging his hands into the tub, Mirchi reached out for a turtle. He stared at the tiny creature, smaller than his palm, and ran a finger over its shell. Then he bent down and released it in the river. Flapping its little flippers, the turtle disappeared under the surface.

Meera and Malhar followed suit, filled with a sense of fulfilment as they watched the little creatures swim away.

'I also have some good news to give you,' said Akhila, as she clicked pictures to remember this moment.

'Just this morning, the Fisheries Department issued a notification banning the use of trawlers along the coastline of Maulsari! It's a big win for sea turtle conservation.'

'Fantastic!' Vanaja Narula exhaled hard. 'I haven't been happier in days.'

'Let's celebrate this New Year then, with a jungle safari,' smiled the SSP. 'I might be able to squeeze in a holiday or two and now that I've been inside, I'm totally smitten.'

'No better way to bring in the New Year than with the team that worked on Operation M4,' smiled the DCF.

'Operation what?' asked Meera.

Smiling, Vanaja Narula exchanged glances with Shekhar and Babu. 'Every operation is given a name for official purposes and communication,' she explained, putting her arm around the children. 'This operation had been given a code too,' she handed them a scroll from her bag, then rubbed Munna's sides. 'In honour of you four, in the official files of the Forest Department, this mission shall always be referred to as Operation M4!'

'Bravo bravo!' clapped the SSP. 'Well done, M4!'

End Note

THE LAW

This story throws light on some aspects of Indian law, as also police and court procedure in India. While the provisions discussed in the story reflect the legal position when the book was published, readers should be aware that laws are territorial and change over time. Further, this book is a work of fiction for young readers, and is not intended to be a reference on Indian law.

WILDLIFE POACHING

Hunting as a human activity, goes back to ancient times. But today, illegal wildlife trade is one of 'the world's largest criminal activities,' as per the Interpol (International Criminal Police Organisation). Annually, the animal trafficking industry is estimated to be worth about $ 20 billion.

India enacted a law in 1972 called the Wildlife (Protection) Act under which hunting of all wildlife is prohibited. However, hunting and illegal wildlife trade continue to take place, driven by various factors—from demand for pets to desire for luxury items, for use as ingredients in traditional medicine to use in black magic rituals. Stones, snares, nets, guns—poachers hunt down animals like tigers, rhinos, elephants, pangolins, birds and snakes, using a range of cruel methods that cause them a lot of suffering. For instance, spotted owlets are passed off as horned owls by inserting red colour into their eyes and pasting their feathers with latex. Illegal wildlife trade takes place today not just through porous international borders, but also openly on the Internet.

YOU CAN HELP TOO!

Perhaps you feel there is little you can do to tackle a problem as large-scale as wildlife poaching. But the truth is, we can all do our bit.

To begin with, make an informed choice about what you consume—be it food, clothes, accessories or cosmetics.

Be a responsible tourist; avoid visiting places that use animals for entertainment or where birds and animals are caged, trapped or chained. Think twice about the source of the curios you buy, like bird feathers or coral jewellery.

If you really want to get a pet, read up about the pet business and choose your pet wisely.

Most of all, make some time to learn about the wildlife around you—the trees and flowers, reptiles and birds. After all, you cannot care about something and save it, when you don't know about it.

Acknowledgements

I thank Arun Venkataramanan of Forest Way, and Students Sea Turtle Conversation Network, for introducing me to the world of turtles. Arun's legendary turtle walks in Chennai led me down a rabbit hole of discovery about turtle and wildlife conversation.

A big thank you to Madhuri Ramesh, Professor at Azim Premji University, Bangalore for going through the manuscript with such enthusiasm and getting back with inputs about turtles and turtle poaching, enabling me to present the issue accurately.

A huge thank you to Shyam Divan, Senior Advocate, Supreme Court of India, and author, *Environmental Law and Policy in India* for his inputs on the manuscript, his encouragement and appreciation.

Thanks are due to Vijay Hiremath, Advocate, Bombay High Court, for being my reference guide on matters of criminal law and procedure.

I am grateful to A. Shankaran, IFS, for chatting with me about life with the Indian Forest Service, its thrills and its challenges.

To my son Kabir, who read this as an eight-year-old, and told me it was one of the best stories he'd read, I owe a great debt. Although child-like and perhaps biased, those words were hugely encouraging; fuelling me through many manuscript rejections.

I am also thankful to the authors of various books (too many to mention here), whose work gave me a glimpse into the murky world of wildlife poaching, the conservation scene in India, and the history of forest laws. As also to the work of organizations like TRAFFIC for their in-depth reports on illegal wildlife trade; Land Conflict Watch, for their detailed reports about conflict over forest land and rights of forest-dwellers in India; and Last Wilderness Foundation, for a peek into the life of Pardhis through their efforts in reducing man-animal conflict in the jungles of Madhya Pradesh.

I thank Sudeshna Shome Ghosh, my editor at Talking Cub, for placing her faith in this series of legal mysteries.

To my family and circle of friends who are the source of much succour—from critical inputs to constant encouragement—words will never be enough to convey my gratitude.

Have you read Book 1
of the M4's adventures?

An M4 MYSTERY BOOK 1

THE CASE OF THE

Vanishing GODS

MALLIKA RAVIKUMAR

Coming soon!

Book 3 of the M4's exciting adventures!